PILLARS OF STEEL

HOW REAL MEN DRAW **STRENGTH** FROM EACH OTHER

BRIAN J. PLACHTA

PRINCIPIA
MEDIA

Pillars of Steel
© 2012 Brian J. Plachta
Published by Principia Media, LLC, Wyoming, MI
www. principiamedia.com

All rights reserved. No part of this book may be reproduced or transmitted in any form by any means, electronic or mechanical, including photocopying and recording, or by any information storage and retrieval system, except as may be expressly permitted by the 1976 Copyright Act or by the publisher. Requests for permission should be made in writing to:
Principia Media, LLC
1853 R W Berends Drive SW
Wyoming, MI 49519

ISBN: 978-1-61485-300-8

Scripture quotations taken from THE MESSAGE. Copyright © by Eugene H. Peterson 1993, 1994, 1995, 1996, 2000, 2001, 2002. Used by permission of NavPress Publishing Group.

The names, characters, places, and incidents in *Pillars of Steel* are either products of the author's imagination or used fictitiously. All characters are fictional and any similarity to people living or dead is purely coincidental.

17 16 15 14 13 12   7 6 5 4 3 2 1

Printed in the United States of America

Cover Design: Frank Gutbrod
Interior Layout: Virginia McFadden

DEDICATION

Pillars of Steel is dedicated to the Spirit of God waiting to be unleashed in all men.

ACKNOWLEDGMENTS

"When God gives you a gift, receive it, savor it like a good cup of tea, lift it up with gratitude to God, and then let it go," my first spiritual director Charm Kulczyk used to tell me.

Gratitude. It's the only word big enough to hold the gift of all those who have helped *Pillars of Steel* come to life. First, thank you to my wife, Denise, my soul mate—your love, support, and daily encouragement have been a pure gift and inspiration as I wrote this book. Thanks for creating the sacred space and freedom I needed to write. You truly are a sign and symbol of God's unconditional love and presence in my life. I love you from the top of my head to the bottom of my heart.

To my children, Matthew, Daniel, Stephen, and Mary Claire and my daughter-in-law Anne—you are gifts from God to me in so many ways. You encouraged me to dream big enough to write *Pillars of Steel*. You have taught me how to laugh and not take life so seriously. You've also shown me how to give and receive love. I am so proud of who you are—each one of you. I see the fingerprints of God all over your lives.

Thank you to my editors, Jane Harradine and Jason Hubbard, who plodded through the drafts of *Pillars of Steel* continuing to encourage me like a blade of grass to "grow." To my spiritual friends and buddies, Jake Delffs, Than Johnson, Ralph Annunziata, Ben Gillis, Fred Cariano and Joseph Byrd—you guys are the true Pillars of Steel who have always had my back, loved me with the kind of philia love guys are meant to share, and are true gifts from God to my heart. Jake Delffs, you will never know how much your words, "You are a writer," changed my life. Thanks for believing in me, when I didn't believe in myself.

The staff and attorneys of my law firm, Plachta, Murphy & Associates, P.C., have been a blessing in allowing me to play hooky on Fridays to write, research, and access the creative spirit within me. I really wasn't just playing golf guys. Miles Murphy III and Bryan Reeder, you are great attorneys, business partners, and friends. It is a privilege to practice law with you. Tracey Boersma, thanks for the words of inspiration that seemed to always come just at the right time to lift me up and dust off my spirit.

Thank you to my spiritual directors over the years, Charm Kulczyk, Sister Nancy Brousseau, O.P., and Don Heydens. You helped me hear the voice of God as you sat month-after-month and watched him have his way with me and in me. The Holy Spirit of God lives and breathes in and through you!

And a huge thanks to the Principia team: Dirk Wierenga, Julie Hurley, and Vern Jones. Your sage-like wisdom in shaping and forming Pillars of Steel has been unbelievable. It is clear that God put each of you into my life at the right time and place. Thanks for being there and for helping dreams come true.

Thank you also to my parents, Joe and Maureen Plachta. You always said that there were two things you hoped you gave your children: love and faith in God. Thank you for giving me both.

And finally God—how do you thank someone or something that is just too darn big to get your arms around and give a big hug? Perhaps the best way is to acknowledge you, heavenly dad, as the source of all gifts. You have always been a gentle and loving father to me. Thanks for loving me first. To you be all glory and honor forever.

Table of Contents

Foreword ix
Introduction:
Man's Quest for Wholeness xi

Chapter 1
What Is the Crisis of Masculinity? 1
Chapter 2
Case Study: One Man's Search for Masculinity 11
Chapter 3
Reclaiming the Past to Shape the Future 20
Chapter 4
Where Did All My Friends Go? 34
Chapter 5
Breaking the Man Code to Become a Man 39
Chapter 6
What Do Men Really Want?—Deep Male Connection 43
Chapter 7
Spiritual Friendships—A Blast from the Past 50
Chapter 8
Implications for Ministry 68
Chapter 9
An End and a Beginning 77

Appendix 1
Order for Making Brothers 79
Appendix 2
A Morning of Conversation
   and Reflection on Men's Spirituality 82

End Notes 85
Bibliography 99
About the Author 102

Foreword

To no one's surprise, given its title, *Pillars of Steel* is a book about men. It is especially helpful for men who have grown tired of stereotypical sitcom jokes where the man is depicted as an insensitive, overbearing buffoon who only discusses sports and women—those who ascribe to the so-called "man code."

Instead, *Pillars of Steel* is a book for men who are looking for a masculine identity in the context of friendships based on something more than one-upmanship or discussing their "latest conquest."

For author Brian Plachta, the search for meaningful dialogue among men has been his quest. After years of quiet reflection, demanding study and exhaustive research—along with seeking answers to his own deeper questions—he shares his findings in *Pillars of Steel*. In it he writes about the hunger for significant relationships in the company of other men as they "develop and deepen their relationship with God."

He invites us to join him in the conversation about the masculine journey, to see how it squares with our own deeper longings. In addition, he provides a framework for discussion that helps men develop the vocabulary to find meaning in today's world.

Pillars of Steel explores the male desire for wholeness while describing the current crisis of masculinity. Patriarchy is dead. Women have stepped forward to take their rightful role. Similarly, for many reasons, men's roles are also changing begging the question: Where does that leave men today?

One of the greatest contributions *Pillars of Steel* offers is its exploration of the history of men's friendships with men, both in classical and religious history. The scriptural word philia (one of the Greek words for love or friendship) is explored in detail. One wonders how such a wonderful concept and practice got lost in the shuffle of history.

Plachta's own pursuit to break "the man code" peaks in the chapter entitled "Breaking the Man Code to Become a Man." It's at once scary, humorous, and challenging. In tackling the raw nerves embedded in such a controversial subject, he shows his ability to be equally at ease talking about sports-friends as he is about male, non-sexual, intimacy between men.

Pillars of Steel also examines scriptural friendships between men, including those Jesus had with John, Peter and Lazarus—a masculine hermeneutic of the gospels, filled with ideas to reflect upon. Based on these friendships, Plachta sets forth four pillars for establishing healthy spiritual friendships, outlining each in detail.

Plachta concludes with specific activities and initiatives to help men develop spiritual connections with other men, activities which are practical and can be used in almost any setting. He does not favor large gatherings instead suggesting guided prayerful assemblies in which a small group of men come together to look inward, to be vulnerable, and to share from the heart with other men, with a willingness to let the Holy Spirit lead them where it will.

Pillars of Steel is not only useful for men who are personally in search of something deeper, but also for those who are mentors, spiritual directors, spirituality and retreat center leaders, as well as church, parish and youth group leaders.

You may find this a challenging read for any number of reasons. One minute you might be in agreement with each word on the page and the next minute disturbed or deeply challenged.

One thing is for sure. This is not an amateur's emotional foray into a hot-button topic. Rather, it is an assertive (firm and gentle) examination of men's spirituality and friendships with concrete suggestions and directions that can be used as a roadmap to wholeness and pathway toward deeper meaning.

Pillars of Steel is filled with energy, optimism, hope and a "can-do" approach.

—Don Heydens
Spiritual Leader

Introduction:
Man's Quest for Wholeness

Have you seen it? Have you heard it? That searching for *more* of life that is on the minds and mouths of a growing number of men these days. Dissatisfied with the games and toys served up by consumerism and the confusing and conflicting messages men receive from modern culture, men are hungry for deeper purpose and spiritual meaning.[1]

Their restlessness smacks with the same pain and discontent vocalized by the rich young man two thousand years ago when he approached Jesus and asked a simple yet profound question: "Good teacher, what must I do to gain the fullness of life?"[2] In response, Jesus invited the rich young man to "Come, follow me."

Unfortunately, the rich young man had no understanding of what that relationship with Christ would involve. So he walked away, back into his isolationism. He missed the opportunity to receive the gift of his heart's deepest desire: wholeness.

That rich young man stands as an icon for the crossroads where men in our Western culture find themselves today: we can either dig deep by doing the inner work necessary to find and live into a fuller understanding of ourselves, each other, and Christ; or we can walk away, trapped by the numbing effect of our modern culture and all its distractions.

Men might rephrase the rich young man's question differently today, asking: How do I find balance in my life? Why does my life seem so empty, without real purpose? Why do I feel numb—like I am living a life of quiet desperation?[3] Yet, at its core, this growing restlessness within men is driven by the same desire to find and achieve wholeness.

Men's desire to find deeper purpose is fueled by the fact that traditional definitions of what it means to be a man are being challenged and distorted by our culture. The uncertainty caused by these shifting trends, researchers in the area of male spirituality[4] warn, has resulted in men becoming alarmingly isolated emotionally and spiritually from not only other men but from themselves. Hence men, and what it means to be a man, stand at a pivot point in history.[5]

Richard Rohr, a Roman Catholic priest and pioneer in the men's movement, captures the current state of men's dilemma:

> Take a typical woman, educated or uneducated, of most any race or ethnicity, and give her this agenda: "You are not to have any close friends or confidants; you are to avoid any show of need, weakness or tender human intimacy; you may not touch other women without very good reason; you may not cry; you are not encouraged to trust your inner guidance but only outer authorities and 'big' people; and you are to judge yourself by your roles, titles, car, house, money and successes. People are either in your tribe, or they are a competitive threat—or of no interest. Then tell her, 'This is what it feels like to be a male, most of the time.'"[6]

"Maleness," reports Rohr, "can be a very lonely and self-defeating world."[7]

Several authors suggest that the crisis in masculinity is further fed by the plague of "misandry"—the Greek term for man-hatred.[8] According to Patrick M. Arnold, S.J., a Jesuit priest who has written extensively about male spirituality, misandry is a form of male-bashing that has arisen as a backlash to the many, and very real, injuries women have received historically from men.

Misandry, Arnold reports, has become mainstream humor. For example, it has become politically correct and socially acceptable to openly engage in negative and derogatory remarks about men as a gender. Such remarks, which might include "Men are all alike" or "All they want is sex" would not be acceptable in today's culture if made about women or any ethnic group. However, these seemingly innocuous comments roll off the tongues of both men and women without concern for how they denigrate males.

Arnold reports that misandry is only now materializing in a few English dictionaries to mirror the opposite term of "misogyny," which is the hatred of women. He defines the term:

Mis*an*dry (mis'-an'-dre) n. hatred of men. 1: the attribution of negative qualities to the entire male gender. 2: the claim that masculinity is the source of human vices such as domination, violence, oppression, and racism. 3: a sexist assumption that (a) male genes, hormones, and physiology, or (b) male cultural nurturing produces war, rape, and physical abuse. 4: the assignment of blame solely to men for humanity's historical evils without including women's responsibility or giving men credit for civilization's achievements. 5: the assumption that any male person is probably dominating, oppressive, violent, sexually abusive, and spiritually immature.[9]

Misandry is a form of sexism. It takes on many shapes and sizes. For example, a college that offers a master's degree in women's studies fails to offer men's studies; flippant remarks left uncorrected, such as, "Men don't know which head they are talking from"; and utterances made which are blatantly derogatory and condemn men as a gender.

Women are also becoming increasingly alarmed by the crisis facing men and boys. Syndicated columnist Suzanne Fields recently posted this editorial opinion in an article titled "When Manly Virtue Died":

> These are difficult and perilous times for boys. A distorted culture has robbed them of virtue to measure themselves against. The good once associated with masculinity in a patriarchal society has been tossed out with the bad. This, alas, is the era of feminist ascendency.
>
> Manhood is more easily mocked, satirized and derided, or exposed for its villainy, exploitation and criminality, than held up as an ideal for boys to aspire to. We've always had rogues, rascals and villains, but until now we've also had a common denominator of what it means to be a man. Male-female cultural distinctions, once blurred, are now disappearing.[10]

This disrespect of men and the gifts they offer society is taking its toll not only on men individually but also on Western culture as a whole. Men are disengaging from the roles through which they have traditionally supported society and its members. According to Arnold, this breakdown of masculinity in America is of great concern to our society since most of our major cultural problems relate in some way to the collapse of masculinity: homelessness, crime, drug addiction, divorce, single-parent families, gang warfare, and so on. On an individual level, many men are also beginning to recognize the masculine crisis in their own lives in the form of father-wounds, alienation, emptiness in their work, collapsed relationships, and loneliness, to name a few.[11]

Arnold maintains that the problem is further complicated by what he calls the "great divorce" between men and Christian spirituality.[12] According to Arnold, one of the greatest obstacles to men's identification with Christianity is that the church's contemporary worship style has taken on a distinctively feminine nature, a flavor with which many men cannot relate.[13] As a result, men increasingly dislike going to church and are dropping out of organized religion at an alarming rate.[14]

Arnold contends Western religion has also abandoned its ancient role of initiating young men into manhood. In fact, the only institution that currently initiates men into manhood through a formal rite of passage is the military. The result, according to psychotherapist and spiritual director Mark Walstrom, is that men are losing their heart, their strength, and their male spirit, leaving them feeling lost, fragmented, and alone.[15]

Notwithstanding these dark times, the call for transformation by and between men is slowly building. According to Walstrom, men's pain and uncertainty about their identity and role as men have forced them to become increasingly intentional about their inner growth. In response to the crisis of masculinity, Arnold observes, "Millions of men are making the choices that lead to new growth, doing the hard and even painful spiritual work, abandoning outmoded roles and superficial identities, adjusting to the liberation of women, and exploring their human potentials. The spiritual growth of men is an inevitable wave into the foreseeable future. The question is, will the church wake up to this tide and plunge into it to help men stay afloat? Or will it draw up its skirts and flee to the shore, convincing itself that all of this uproar is yet another 'Modern Bad Thing.'"[16]

Some researchers suggest that the growth of the current men's movement is part of the rebalancing of human nature. Author Carol Lee Flinders, in her book *Rebalancing the World*, suggests that the ongoing pendulum swing is indicative of the movement toward restoring the mutuality of relationships between men and women. She contends that the women's movement of the 1960s and the current men's movement, which began in the 1980s, are both part of a cultural reshaping. This reforming will ultimately establish equilibrium between men and women individually, in relationship with each other, and in relationship with God and creation.[17]

Hence, the tension in modern culture surrounding the crisis of men and the shifting definitions of what it means to be a man are simply a natural and evolving part of reshaping masculinity. This reshaping will require the following types of men:

> **1. Trailblazers.** Men's leaders must rise up, gear up, and become the trailblazers willing to call other men toward the courageous path of doing the inner work necessary to redefine themselves, both individually and culturally, much like women did during the 1960s with the advent of the women's movement.
>
> **2. Toolbox Tenders.** Men's pastoral counselors must study, understand, and embrace the new tools and insights arising out of the men's movement to help men do their inner work.
>
> **3. Transformers.** Most importantly, men individually, and in the company of other men, must follow the path of the sage and hero, becoming men with the strength and courage to embrace the quest to seek and find their masculine souls so they can gain the inner wholeness they seek.

For too long, men have walked the hero's journey alone, spurning the company of other men. One crucial factor in resolving the current crisis in masculinity is a return to the unique vision that came from the wisdom of the early church fathers through a doctrine written about extensively during the fifth through twelfth centuries by such men as Augustine and Anselm. The doctrine is that of "Spiritual Friendship."[18] The concept is simple, yet profound: men whose hearts are united by the Spirit of God in divine friendship that brings men together toward the common pursuit of the One, the Eternal Friend.[19] The impact of reigniting this vision for men could well be transformative, not only for individual men but for society as a whole.[20]

In seeking to reclaim this tool from the ancient past, we will examine the following questions:

- How do we define the current crisis of masculinity in Western culture and in the Christian church, and how did this crisis happen?
- What are the historical and theological roots of the doctrine of spiritual friendship and how was this type of friendship lost and abandoned?
- How can the doctrine of spiritual friendship provide new vision and tools for pastoral counseling with men in today's culture?
- What are the implications for ministry and pastoral counseling?

The ancient doctrine of spiritual friendship is a valuable gift that men and pastoral counselors can reclaim. These spiritual friendships may very well prove to be an invaluable tool for men to help them build a vastly deeper spiritual and psychological foundation. As men redefine their unique role in society and find deeper wholeness within and through their relationships with other men, they will strengthen society and continue to be transformed into the image and likeness of God.[21]

At the end of this book, we will examine a model for building community among men relying heavily on the theology of spiritual friendships. We will highlight the urgent need in our culture and in the church to return to the doctrine of spiritual friendships and the theology of friendship as an important tool for men's transformation. To begin, let's examine how the crisis in masculinity occurred.

CHAPTER 1
WHAT IS THE CRISIS OF MASCULINITY?

"A crisis is a terrible thing—and it's about time we had one!" declares Inspector Kemp in a line from the popular movie *Young Frankenstein*. But what is a crisis? And how can we say modern men face a crisis in terms of their masculinity? More importantly, is there a paradox within this crisis, so that the crisis itself is the fuel igniting men to seek and find true manhood with its gift of wholeness?

The term *crisis* derives its definition from the Greek word *krisein*, which means "to choose." Men and society have made a choice to abandon the past patriarchal definitions of manhood. Yet, we have failed to replace them with new healthy concepts of what it means culturally and spiritually to be a man and live out one's authentic masculinity. Hence, we are in the midst of the death and rebirth cycle inherent within a crisis as we struggle with the question: what *does* true masculinity mean?

The existence of the current crisis in masculinity is well documented. In its July/August 2010 edition, *Atlantic* reporter Hanna Rosin boldly declared in an article titled "The End of Men" that matriarchy has now replaced patriarchy, and man's last stand may be upon us.[22] Rosin made her unprecedented declaration based on recent reports which indicated that the number of women in the United States workforce had surpassed that of men. According to Rosin:

> Earlier this year, for the first time in American history, the balance of the workforce tipped toward women, who now hold a majority of the nation's jobs. The working class, which has long defined our notions of masculinity, is slowly turning into a matriarchy, with men increasingly absent from the home and women making all the decisions.[23]

This man-is-at-his-end prognosis smacks like a whip sharp and loud across the backs of men. This diagnosis is as monumental as *Time* magazine's 1966 assertion that "God is dead."[24]

Following the *Atlantic*'s lead, *Newsweek* magazine joined the fray with its September 20, 2010, edition featuring an article titled "What's the Matter with Men?"[25] The author attributed the "decline of men" to such factors as the Great Recession and the shifting definitions of manhood rising and falling over the past decade. These shallow, revolving-door descriptions of masculinity include:

The old macho. The return to the old definitions of masculinity: strong, in control and insensitive, as often depicted by actor John Wayne.

The metro sexual man. A heterosexual man with a strong interest in fashion and appearance.

The retro sexual man. A heterosexual man who spends as little money as possible on his personal appearance and lifestyle because he has very little interest in how he looks and what he wears.

The techno sexual man. A metro sexual man who, as well as being concerned with fashion and appearance, has a strong interest in technology.[26]

In an over-simplified attempt to resolve the current debate over what it means to be a man in our culture, *Newsweek* demands culture adopt the "new macho." The "new macho," according to *Newsweek*, requires men to have paternity leave, spend more time with their children, do more housework, and pursue traditionally female-dominated professions like nursing and teaching.

Television has also joined the decline-of-man bandwagon over the past decade. A quick channel surf through the most popular television stations soon confirms that many shows commonly depict male characters as what one media watch organization terms "the **buffoon**"—a bungling father figure in TV ads and sitcoms. These men are usually well-intentioned and light-hearted characters, ranging from slightly inept to completely hopeless when it comes to parenting their children or dealing with domestic or workplace issues.[27]

The media hoopla over the alleged decline of men recently stirred a backlash among those in the front lines of the men's movement. Boysen Hodgson, one of the leaders of the Mankind Project, a men's ministry group, wrote a rebuttal to the *Newsweek* article, which is reprinted below:

The New Macho
He cleans up after himself. He cleans up the planet. He is a role model for young men. He is rigorously honest and fiercely optimistic.

He holds himself accountable. He knows what he feels. He knows how to cry and he lets it go. He knows how to rage without hurting others. He knows how to fear and how to keep moving. He knows self-mastery.

He's let go of childish shame. He feels guilty when he's done something wrong. He is kind to men, kind to women, kind to children. He teaches others how to be kind. He says he's sorry.

He stopped blaming women or his parents or men for his pain years ago. He stopped letting his defenses ruin his relationships. He stopped letting his penis run his life. He has enough self-respect to tell the truth. He creates intimacy and trust with his actions. He has men that he trusts and that he turns to for support. He knows how to roll with it. He knows how to make it happen. He is disciplined when he needs to be. He knows how to listen from the core of his being.

He's not afraid to get dirty. He's ready to confront his own limitations. He has high expectations for himself and for those he connects with. He looks for ways to serve others. He knows he is an individual. He knows that we are all one. He knows he is an animal and a part of nature. He knows his spirit and his connection to something greater.

He knows that the future generations are watching his actions. He builds communities where people are respected and valued. He takes responsibility for himself and is also willing to be his brother's keeper.

He knows his higher purpose.
He loves with fierceness.
He laughs with abandon, because he gets the joke.[28]

Two important core questions arise from the end-of-men debate:

Is modern man truly on the decline or even at his end, or are men instead in the midst of a major paradigm shift (called the men's movement), much like women experienced as a result of the women's movement in the 1960s?

If the latter is the case, will a new and perhaps more authentic model of manhood emerge from the rubble of men's current upheaval?

Society, it seems, is currently wrestling out loud with these and similar questions while the old paradigms of masculinity slowly give way to new emerging ones. As we wait for these new templates to form, be shaped, and integrated into our culture, the conversation can be furthered best by scholars who are willing to examine the past and honor those aspects of men's history and masculinity which have been traditionally helpful to men and society. Such an intellectual look back, outside of the media hoopla, will help us more fully understand how men "got here" from "there."

How did we get here from there?

Robert Bly in his epic 1990 book on masculinity titled *Iron John*,[29] provides a historical perspective on how men arrived at the doorstep of the current men's movement. By examining Western culture through the lens of the shifting cultural definitions and models of manhood, he defines the following significant periods of modern man:

The Fifties Male

Bly suggests that in the 1950s, the agreed upon model for an American man both in society and in our churches was the male who dutifully got to work early, labored responsibly, and supported his wife and children with admired discipline.[30] Ronald Reagan, Bly reports, is the "mummified version of this dogged type."

Many of the fifties male qualities were strong and positive. However, underneath the charm and bluff was—and remains even in today's male—much "isolation, deprivation, and passivity."[31] In fact, Bly says, unless this type of man has an enemy, he isn't sure that he is alive.

The fifties man was supposed to like football, be aggressive, be staunchly patriotic, never cry, and always provide. The fifties man had a clear vision of what a man was and what his responsibilities were, yet lived a life of isolation and one-sided vision, which were extremely dangerous for him and for society.[32]

The Vietnam Era and the Women's Movement

During the 1960s, with the outbreak and violence of the Vietnam War, the male cookie cutter defining masculinity became visibly broken. The waste and violence of the Vietnam War caused men to question their vision of what it meant to be a man. If being a man meant Vietnam, the sixties male wasn't sure he wanted any part of manhood as we had known it for generations.

Alongside the Vietnam War, the feminist movement emerged, questioning the patriarchal society we had inherited from previous generations. Men began to examine women's history and their sensitivity. As a result, many men began to notice their "feminine side" and pay more attention to their emotions and feelings. This process, according to Bly, continues to this day. Most contemporary men have been transformed in some way by the women's movement.[33]

Bly suggests that the women's movement has had a positive impact on men by encouraging men to become more nurturing, thoughtful, and gentle. But Bly warns this development in male character has not made men more free. Instead, men have become symbolized as the nice boy who pleases his wife and his mother.

The fact that the women's movement has deeply impacted and caused significant changes in the traditional definitions of masculinity is well supported by the work of modern researchers. According to professor of sociology Peter M. Nardi, definitions of masculinity are historically reactive to changing definitions of femininity. Thus, when changes occurred in how work was organized and how the family was structured, women's roles entered the public sphere and femininity was redefined. "Given the relational nature of gender, masculinity in turn began to be reconstructed."[34]

The Sexual Revolution of the Sixties

The sexual revolution of the sixties in Western culture resulted in the collapse of the four traditional forms of love recognized by ancient Greeks into one form of love, eros. Ancient Greek writing has long emphasized that there are four distinct types of love: agape, eros, philia, and storge. *Agape* (unconditional love) is characterized by the unconditional love God has for humankind. *Eros* (romantic love) is a sensual love with deep desire and longing. *Philia* (friendship) is typified by brotherly love. It is a virtuous love which includes loyalty, equality, and familiarity. *Storge* (affection) connotes natural fondness like that felt by parents for a child. It is typically found in connection with family relationships.[35]

The sexual revolution of the sixties looked at human nature solely through the lens of sex—discussed as erotic love, or eros. This primary emphasis on eros, fueled by Freud's writings suggesting that human beings are motivated solely out of a sexually driven context, resulted in the loss of the concept of *philia* love. Hence, Bly contends, *philia* love quickly collapsed into eros. And since there was no longer a container for men to express love for another man, the expression of male affection for another male became viewed as solely erotic.

Disguised glimpses of socially acceptable forms of *philia*—brotherly love—continue to a limited degree, but typically only in the context of sports or the military. These watered-down forms of male friendships are staunchly governed by the "man rules," the unwritten code of social conduct discussed further below, which restricts men's interactions with each other. Hence, men's relationships with each other have become and continue to be strictly limited to competition, task cooperation, and "buddy-ship."[36]

According to Christian ethics professor James B. Nelson, with this collapse of *philia* love into *eros*, men were without a cultural foundation to safely experience any sense of intimacy between themselves and other men for fear of being labeled homosexual.[37]

The Seventies Soft Male

The trend arising out of the women's movement which encouraged men to become more sensitive and in touch with their emotions led to what Bly calls the "soft male" of the seventies.[38] The soft males of the seventies are men who are lovely, valuable people, but are not happy, because they have lost their strength and freedom. They are life-preserving, but not exactly life-giving.[39] "Now we have a finely tuned young man, ecologically superior to his father, sympathetic to the whole harmony of the universe, yet he himself has little vitality to offer," Bly writes.[40] This loss of strength has caused a dramatic shift in the definition of masculinity to the extent that men and women now seriously question what it means to be a man in the current century.

In the midst of this confusion and conflicting attempts to redefine masculinity, men's spirituality author David Murrow notes that the "soft male" mentality has now spilled over from society into the church. According to Murrow, our Christian church culture now expects men to be the "Christian nice guy"—people-pleasing men who try to lead, but have no backbone. Lacking strength, they are too "gentle, meek and passive."[41]

This trend has led to a feminization of the church both in worship and in leadership style. As a result, men no longer identify with the changing experience of church. Becoming disconnected, their participation in organized religion is rapidly declining. Additionally, the failure of the church to provide meaningful rituals for boys to be initiated into manhood has caused men to question what relevance, if any, the church plays in their daily life.[42]

In contrast to the various new and conflicting models of masculinity, Murrow suggests that the model of the perfect man, as characterized by the life of Christ, is the authentic model of manhood men are being invited to integrate into their masculinity in the midst of the current crisis. In order to become like Christ, Murrow suggests, men must do the inner soul work necessary to develop three key masculine virtues: submission, strength, and sacrifice.[43] Murrow contends that men have done a good job in learning to be submissive, i.e., humble, and to sacrifice for their families and loved ones. However, they have lost the virtue of strength because of their own abuse of it.

As a result of this historical abuse of power—and women's demand for equality—society has rejected patriarchy as a norm, casting away its old tenets which had suggested men were superior to women and had the right and obligation to hold cultural control. While this rebalancing of power between men and women has had a positive impact on society, the pendulum shift has swung too far in the opposite direction toward a staunch matriarchy, with its resulting misandry, according to both Bly and Murrow. Thus, further rebalancing and re-centering is inevitable.

Instead of being respected for being a strong male, men are now often ridiculed for exercising their strength and are depicted as weak and powerless. This feminization of men will require men to find and regain a proper balance of strength tempered with wisdom and compassion as one of their core virtues. Hence, in order to grow into the fullness of their manhood, men in our culture must reclaim their strength as a natural part of their male spirit. To avoid abusing that strength once again, however, men must root their manhood in the servant leadership model evidenced by the life of Christ.[44]

The Deep Male and the Men's Movement

Despite the upheaval prompted in part by shifting definitions of manhood, the experience of American men over the last three decades as they walk through this current period of redefining masculinity has been valuable in several respects:

Men have been able to open up emotionally to discover and embrace their unique male spirit and character.

The abuses of a strict patriarchal society have been eliminated or at least significantly reduced.

Men are increasingly seeking more balance in their lives, discovering their gifts, following their deep passions and authentic desires.

This is not the final stop for men, however, according to Bly. Rather, much more travel lies ahead. The trek needed is what Bly calls the "deep male" journey. This journey to a man's inner core provides each man with an exciting challenge to integrate their male strength with their new-found sensitivity, reclaiming and rebalancing the lost parts of genuine manhood discarded during the cultural shift from the 1960s to the present.

The emergence of the "deep male" is a phoenix rising from the dust of the last three decades, where traditional models of manhood were abandoned without proper replacements. With patriarchy now dismissed as a cultural norm, a man no longer needs to live the lonely, isolated, macho man style of the fifties (which was often harmful and oppressive to women); nor does he have to live as a soft male, fashioned out of the last thirty years (which has proved harmful to men). Instead, modern man has been freed to take the inner journey into the deep male, that dark spiritual place of a man's psyche where the epic hero appears as a man discovers his emerging masculine energy.[45]

The deep male is the man who has the courage to explore his inner self, to look at the wet, dark places of his soul. The deeply masculine man is willing to embrace his "wild man" energy and make the necessary changes in his life, not out of brashness and knee-jerk reaction, but out of firm resolve and desire.

This emerging male is willing and eager to let other men teach him wisdom and to find his own wisdom by reflecting on his life experiences to see what they have to teach him. He is willing to let his life speak to him.

The deep male is willing to be vulnerable, because he knows that it is through his brokenness he finds healing and direction, where he finds the spiritual values and integrity to live. Making contact with this deep male, the wild man finds his new power in grace as he regains balanced masculine strength.[46] The deep male discovers his inner spirit, the spirit St. Paul calls: the inner man.[47]

Bly's deep male energy has many of the qualities poetically depicted by Boysen Hodgson in his New Macho reflection reprinted above. This New Macho is the spirit of a hero willing to plunge into the inner sea of his life, looking for enlightenment, trusting that what he will find within himself is indeed the pearl of great price. This is a man's warrior spirit willing to search inside himself to seek and find inner riches. The deep male is the embodiment of the merchant described by Christ in the parable of the pearl: "Again, the Kingdom of Heaven is like a man who is a merchant seeking fine pearls, who having found one pearl of great price, he went and sold all that he had, and bought it."[48] The spirit of the deep male is symbolized by Jesus praying through his fear in the garden of Gethsemane, St. Joseph mentoring his son in the carpenter's shop, and Job finding wisdom in the midst of his suffering.

The deep male is the inner man which the rich young man was looking for when he asked Christ to show him how to find eternal life. What he was seeking was inside himself all the time. He just refused to abandon worldly distractions to find his true self buried deep within his masculine soul.

Current historians of the men's movement as well as men's spirituality experts agree that the rediscovery of the deep male inside each man is the next step for men in modern society. It is the epic journey all men must take to find wholeness. The deep male has various names: the New Macho, the Wild Man, Iron John, and St. Paul in Ephesians 3:16 calls him the "Inner Man."

Regardless of what name is used to describe this emerging male spirit, each term points men in the same direction: toward doing the necessary soul work men must do to rediscover their inner self.[49]

In an effort to see how this inner soul work is done, let's examine one man's epic journey, where his willingness to hold his brokenness alongside his strength became the tool that successfully helped him tackle his haunting masculinity issues.

Chapter 2
Case Study: One Man's Search for Masculinity

Luke, at age forty-six, had three issues in his life he could not seem to reconcile: a demanding professional career that he describes was "sucking the life blood" from him; a sense of calling to do more with his life in some form of ministry; and a life-long struggle with what he characterized as same-sex attraction.[50] Happily married for over twenty years to a loving and supportive wife and the father of three healthy children, Luke couldn't understand why he was often drawn to the Internet to look at pictures of strong and athletic men.

Luke's father died when Luke was seven. The youngest of six siblings, Luke was quickly plunged into the role of being the caretaker for his mother, since his older siblings had already left home to pursue college and their own careers. While still reeling from his own loss, his focus quickly shifted to helping his mother deal with the devastation of putting her life back together after thirty-five years of a codependent marriage.

Consistent with the strong unemotional personality his father had modeled for him, Luke soon pulled himself up by the bootstraps, thrusting head on into the adult role of a surrogate husband while still a child. His tough personality, which masked his inner fear, allowed him to tend to the needs of his mother, complete high school, and move on to finish second in his accounting class. His bull-like mentality drove him to become a partner in his accounting firm in five years, rather than the typical seven-year track, and to become a pillar of leadership in his church, where he served as the chairman of the parish council and head of a lay ministry team.

Despite all the outward success in his life, Luke said he felt empty, isolated, and angry at himself for having these unwanted attractions to other men. His life felt dualistic. On the outside he looked like the all-American male whose dreams of a great career, loving wife, and successful children had come true, yet on the inside he felt like a failure and a hypocrite.

Luke had no close male friends in his life. Instead, he said his wife was his best friend. He'd had several close drinking buddies throughout high school and college. However, once he began his family and career, there simply was no spare time to invest in meaningful friendships. Yet, he yearned for male companionship in a way he couldn't define.

Despite his strong urges, Luke had not acted out with other men. Having grown up in a strict Catholic family, he kept his secret buried, only allowing himself to masturbate alone and in private while viewing images of favorite male sports figures and nude models on the Internet.

Prior to coming into spiritual direction to sort through his feelings, Luke questioned whether he was gay. He attended monthly meetings of Courage, a ministry approved by the Roman Catholic Church to help men deal with same-sex attraction ("SSA"). Courage relies upon the twelve steps of Alcoholics Anonymous to help men control their feelings.

Luke found that the Courage group did not help much. Courage treated SSA as an addiction that had to be contained like the thirst for alcohol, he said, so it only made him feel like he was sick. The other guys in the group, led by a Catholic priest, seemed like they were dams ready to burst. Luke was concerned that there were guys in the group trying to hit on each other outside the meetings, which only added to his confusion.

After eight months of meetings, Luke decided the Courage approach wasn't doing him any good, so he stopped attending. This decision left him feeling even more confused, frustrated, and isolated.

Luke prayed to God on a daily basis. In his morning meditation, he would often ask God to either take away his desires or at least give him the ability to live with them with integrity.

One of the counselors in whom Luke had confided told Luke that perhaps this was just a thorn in his side that would never go away. Like St. Paul, he said, Luke would simply have to learn to live with it. That felt cruel to Luke. He reported in one spiritual counseling session, "That doesn't make sense to me. Why would God intentionally place a thorn inside of me to keep me in line? That's not the loving God I have come to know and trust. There must be something more to this."

For years, Luke disciplined himself to keep his behavior controlled and secretive. He continued to view Internet pictures of men, masturbate in private, and then feel a mixed sense of relief and shame for having "given in to lust," he reported. He would often go to the sacrament of reconciliation, confessing the same sin over and over, feeling lost and humiliated because he did not seem to be able to get beyond this issue in his life. He never acted out inappropriately with other men, choosing instead to live within his own secret thoughts and desires haunting him like a ghost.

After decades of quiet frustration, Luke's struggle started coming out sideways. He tried meeting other men through a platonic ad he placed on Craig's List to see if he could find other guys who might have an interest in mutual rubdowns without any sexual component to it.

Luke was able to connect with two other men who also had a deep faith life and struggled with SSA. On several occasions, they exchanged rubdowns, which at times included full body. These connections with other men never involved genital stimulation and did not lead to sexual relations. Rather, Luke found for the first time a healing touch through massage with his buddies that transmitted male strength, acceptance, and support to him.

The friendships often grew deeper on an intellectual and emotional basis as his buddies shared their faith journeys and struggles. Luke and his new-found friends also discussed their wives and children, how much they loved them and wanted to remain faithful to them. The men also found support by emailing each other during the work week with words of encouragement and affirmation. The emails, Luke said, took away much of the loneliness he experienced. They made him feel like "some other guy had your back."

Having no labels other than "bisexual" or "gay" to ascribe to his feelings and new experiences, Luke felt conflicted. On one hand, he felt a unique sense of peace and wholeness from the male acceptance and affirmation he received from his buddies. On the other hand, he felt shame and remorse for nonsexual rubdowns which were a small but important part of the friendships.

Eventually, Luke took on the label of bisexual and fell into a homosexual relationship with another man who had divorced after fifteen years of marriage and had taken on the gay lifestyle. This friendship eventually moved into a sexual relationship, with the exchanges going well beyond the boundaries of mutual rubdowns. Six months into the new friendship, Luke abruptly terminated all contact with the friend, concerned that the relationship had evolved into something he did not want or need in his life.

After cutting off the relationship, Luke decided to abstain from any physical connection with other men, nonsexual or otherwise, including rubdowns. He soon sank into a deep and angry depression. His conflicted heart told him the abstinence was holy, yet he longed for something he still couldn't define. This inner conflict led to roller-coaster emotions as he tried to sort through the issues openly in our spiritual counseling sessions.

In the midst of this turmoil, a turning point occurred in Luke's life. At the end of a long weekend getaway with his wife of twenty years, Luke unexpectedly shared his lifelong struggles with her. Although Luke and his wife had a strong marriage and shared no other secrets, Luke had chosen early on in his marriage not to tell his wife about his struggles with same-sex attraction out of fear she would label him gay and leave him.

However, in a moment of grace that weekend, Luke heard these words silently speak to him: "The truth will set you free." Perhaps because he could no longer live with the inner conflict, surprisingly Luke responded to that voice by spilling out to his wife all of his feelings and past behavior.

Luke's wife was devastated, yet she tried hard to be supportive. She asked Luke point-blank if he was gay. Did he want out of their marriage? Did he still love her? Luke assured her that he did still love her, was not gay, and did not want out of their marriage. He and his wife then openly discussed all of the options available to them. After several long, candid, and difficult conversations, they decided that no matter how messy it was or might become, they would remain committed to each other and their marriage while working through this challenge together with God's help.[51]

The next few months were difficult. Although Luke had shared his experiences and his struggles openly in spiritual direction with me long before he shared them with his wife, as his spiritual director, I had no background or framework to deal with these types of issues. I had never encountered this issue in spiritual direction before—had no textbook, tools, or paradigm to lean into to formulate the questions necessary to help Luke effectively sift and sort through his thoughts and feelings. Therefore, as his spiritual director, I simply sat and listened to Luke month after month, praying the Holy Spirit would help him find the inner healing he so desperately needed.

Each month Luke expressed his deepest desire, which was to follow Christ and live in integrity in the midst of this attraction, which he said felt like a parasite on his soul. Not knowing what else to do for him, I eventually suggested he engage the services of a licensed Christian counselor to help him sort out the psychological dimensions of his father-wound and related masculinity issues.

Sadly, I watched him become more conflicted month after month as the counselor simply tried to get Luke to give voice to his pain and then "give it to Jesus to heal." I grew increasingly confused as a spiritual director about where God and Luke were going with this issue. I even discussed in my peer group that I had never been stretched so far, feeling powerless as a spiritual director, simply having to trust that God would somehow work with his surprising grace through Luke's struggle.

Just as I was about to give up hope and suggest Luke see another spiritual director who might be better equipped to help him, Luke came into our next session remarkably happy. He reported he had connected with a ministry in Florida called In His Fullness and that he had undertaken several one-on-one telephone coaching sessions with the two men who headed the ministry. In His Fullness believes God has hard-wired men to need the company of other men through what they call "*davaq*" friendships. Based on their study of the Bible, eight years of intensive research, and their own personal struggles with masculinity, the In His Fullness team proposes that some men are neither bisexual nor gay. Rather, they are simply looking for the deep male connection found in walking alongside another man as his best friend and confidant.

Based on Ephesians 3:19 and Proverbs 18:24, the In His Fullness (IHF) team coached Luke that God has placed legitimate desires in men that cause a longing in their hearts for genuine and authentic relationships with other men. These *davaq* relationships arise out of God's desire for men to have holistic bonds with other men of integrity in an emotional, intellectual, spiritual, and physical (nonsexual) fashion. These cleaving relationships, similar to that of Jonathan and David, and Jesus and John, are part of God's design for men, the IHF team helped Luke understand. According to IHF, men are not supposed to go through life alone, but rather need the fellowship of other men to help iron sharpen iron and point each other toward God. Culture and society, IHF believes, have sexualized so many parts of life that the only options left for men in our modern times are either one of the following two, neither of which is satisfying or intended by God:

The Lone Wolf Approach
Lead a traditional straight life being lonely, isolated due to our homophobic culture and experience no deep male connections, or at best, only shallow male friendships limited to the "man rules" of safe topics such as women, work, and sports.

Homosexuality
Embrace the gay lifestyle with other men and leave one's wife and children when faced with male attraction.

In His Fullness, according to Luke, offered him the following third option he had never considered:

Spiritual Friendships [52]

Defined as healthy male friendships, similar to foxhole buddies that are founded on the love of Christ, these relationships include four critical pillars of intimate connection between men: (i) intellectual; (ii) emotional; (iii) spiritual; and (iv) physical. These spiritual friendships, if authentic, IHF claims, will point each man toward Christ and wholeness.[53] The intimacy in the friendships is defined as a sharing of one's inner life with one or two other men, something men are often afraid to develop with other guys since the "man rules" limit them to competition, not intimacy, with other men. The physical component is never sexual, but rather respective of the fact that men experience the world in a tangible, physical way.[54]

Luke also indicated he had connected with a new friend who lived nearby who had been studying with the IHF team for the past year and a half. His buddy Joe introduced Luke to a deeper understanding of what God intended for men. He explained how friendships with deep male connections are perhaps what Luke's heart was searching for. His mistake in sexualizing his God-given need for healthy male friendships had now been named, thus losing its power, Luke reported. Luke felt he was finally able to give voice to his true desire: healthy deep male friendships which point each other toward God. As a result, Luke said he felt a freedom to pursue his heart's desire in a holistic way.

The results in Luke's life were remarkable. Over the next six months, he and his wife studied the materials from IHF together to better understand the paradigm proposed by the ministry team. Luke's wife met Joe and his wife, gaining a deeper trust that this friendship was good and one that could follow a road map of proper boundaries—one which would not jeopardize either couple's marriage. With his wife's blessing, Luke also went on two individualized retreats offered by IHF. According to Luke's wife, he came back from those retreats with the masculine strength she knew was always in him but, until now, he couldn't seem to find.

Luke's relationship with his spouse catapulted. They experienced the true oneness they had longed for throughout their twenty years of marriage. With the grace of a spiritual friendship and the willingness to do the hard inner spiritual work and prayer he needed to continue to grow into his true manhood, Luke reported he had found the integrity he was looking for inside himself. More importantly, he has continued to grow and evolve into his "true self," letting go of much of his inner baggage, which was hampering his journey to wholeness. In fact, his life has been so dramatically impacted that he is slowly and prayerfully embarking upon establishing a men's group to help men dealing with these and other spiritual and masculinity issues.

Although Luke reports that there are still moments of doubt which he takes into prayer as he continues to discern whether this new paradigm is "messy grace" or instead from some other unholy spirit, his inner work and willingness to be real with his struggles has led him to a place of genuine masculine strength. He reports he has been able to embrace and integrate what he believes are the three masculine journeys of Christ all men must undertake: submission, strength, and sacrifice.[55]

Luke now rejects the cultural labels of "gay," "straight," or "bisexual." Rather, he reports, he is simply "guy"—a man created by God with the need to walk on the journey alongside one or two other men as friends who are willing to share their hearts and souls and their physical strength with each other, men whose primary purpose is to help each other find their inner self and continue to point their lives toward Christ.

Luke's journal entry, which he shared with me in a recent session, describes the depth of his self-discovery and growing integration:

> "I have finally found what I was looking for—that sense of knowing in my heart and mind that I am a man and have what it takes; that sense of loving my male body and spirit and mind and celebrating it as a gift from God; knowing in my heart that Jesus is the fullest expression of what it means to be a man and I am on the road to wholeness in my own masculinity. Suddenly, I realized that what I have been looking for in another man is my masculinity and he can never give that to me because I have to find it within myself and embrace it as my own gift. And that masculinity is a gift from God. All I have to do is open it and embrace what is already there."

The *davaq* friendship model which Luke embraced skyrocketed his personal growth and maturity. Yet some might claim it is too cutting edge and perhaps countercultural.

Upon closer examination, however, it is clear such friendships are not without historical and theological precedent. In fact, its theological roots are deeply embedded in the theology of spiritual friendship—a tenet of the Christian faith written about extensively by the early church fathers, including Aelred of Rievaulx in his 1147 treatise entitled *Spiritual Friendships*. Its cultural roots are steeped in the ancient Greek definition and celebration of the virtue of *philia*. The Greeks so espoused friendships that they defined them as a highly apprised form of love, claiming it as one of the noblest achievements of human nature.[56]

Despite its widespread historical acceptance and support, as well as its deep theological and cultural roots, the doctrine of spiritual friendship has been virtually abandoned both by the church and modern culture. A growing number of men's groups, however, are beginning to rediscover this ancient tool of spiritual growth.[57]

As Luke discovered, the current paths available for men seem to call for either feast or famine, leading men further away from God instead of closer to him. While Luke admits there are temptations in walking this narrow path, it appears to have huge implications for men and pastoral counseling with men as long its chief focus is on Christ and the grace necessary to sustain the journey toward wholeness.[58]

With Luke's story as background, let's take a look and see if what Luke experienced is consistent with the historical doctrine of spiritual friendship and its companion theology of friendship. If his modern story is consistent with this ancient doctrine, it might very well be that Luke rediscovered a tool for men, as well as for women, which could help them gain a deeper sense of the "fullness of life" sought by the rich young man in Matthew's gospel—a fullness of life being desperately sought by many men today. To begin that examination, let's look at the past to see how it might inform our future.

Chapter 3
Reclaiming the Past to Shape the Future

Prior to the nineteenth century, the concept of love between men akin to brotherly love was a central part of the definition of masculinity.[59] Friendships among men were most highly revered in ancient Greece as well as during the European Renaissance.

The ancient Greeks counted friendship as a preeminent form of love. This virtue, called *philia*, was so esteemed by the Greeks that achieving true *philia* love between two men at the deepest level of friendship was seen as one of the noblest achievements of human nature. It bore an essential relationship to the good and virtuous life.[60] C. S. Lewis captures the Greek spirit concerning *philia* love in this way:

"Few modern people think Friendship a love of comparable value or even a love at all ... To the Ancients, Friendship seemed the happiest and most fully human of all loves; the crown of life and the school of virtue. The modern world, in comparison, ignores it."[61]

The Greek philosopher Cicero wrote extensively about the virtue of friendship as a form of *philia* love in his classic work *De Amicitia*. Cicero divided the essence of friendship into three parts: the nature, advantages, and laws of friendship. Cicero is often cited for his definition of friendship as: "An agreement on matters human and divine, with charity and good will."[62] According to Cicero, true friendships are based on the virtue of love and are something for which every man should strive:

> For man not only loves himself, but seeks another whose spirit he may so blend with his own as almost to make one being of two (Section 21).
>
> It is virtue, virtue which both creates and preserves friendship. On it depends harmony of interest, permanence, fidelity. When Virtue has reared her head and shewn the light of her countenance, and seen and recognized the same light in another,

she gravitates towards it, and in her turn welcomes that which the other has to shew; and from it springs up a flame which you may call love or friendship as you please. Both words are from the same root in Latin; and love is just the cleaving to him whom you love without the prompting of need or any view to advantage, though this latter blossoms spontaneously on friendship, little as you may have looked for it.... And since the law of our nature and of our life is that a new generation is forever springing up, the most desirable thing is that along with your contemporaries, with whom you started in the race, you may also teach what is to us the goal. But in view of the instability and perishableness of mortal things, we should be continually on the look-out for someone to love and by whom to be loved; for if we lose affection and kindliness from our life, we lose all that gives it charm.... (Section 27).

This is all I had to say on friendship. One piece of advice on parting. Make up your minds to this. Virtue (without which friendship is impossible) is first; but next to it, and to it alone, the greatest of all things is Friendship. (Section 27).[63]

According to Cicero, the development of deep friendships is a natural and necessary part of being human. A type of "second self" develops out of one's friendships, which contributes to the well-being of not only the individual but also of society as a whole. For Cicero, true friendship was the second most important quality of being human, second only to the development of virtue in one's life.[64]

Aristotle also wrote extensively on the intrinsic value and virtue of friendship in Books VIII and IX of his treatise on *Ethics*.[65] According to Aristotle, friendship is a relation to some other person or persons without which life is hardly worth living. For Aristotle there is an inseparable relationship between virtuous activity and friendship.

His ethical review of friendships begins with the premise that there are three principal reasons why one person might like someone else as a friend. For example, one might be attracted to another because he is:

Virtuous:
I love my friend because I find him to have a virtuous character to which I seek to aspire and which he draws out of me.

Useful:
I love him because of the ways in which is he useful to me.

Pleasant:
I love him because of the pleasure I get out of him.[66]

The nature of the friendship depends on which of these three qualities binds the friends together. When two individuals recognize that the other person is someone of good character, and they spend time with each other engaged in activities that strengthen their character, then they form the best possible type of friendship. If they are equally virtuous, according to Aristotle, their friendship is perfect.

If, however, there is a large gap in their moral development (as between a parent and a small child, or between a husband and a wife), then although their relationship may be based on the other person's good character, it will be imperfect because of their inequality.[67]

According to Aristotle, the highest form of genuine friendship must be based on the first premise, which is goodness or virtue. Virtuous friendships will by their nature draw both friends into leading happier and more fulfilling lives for their betterment and for that of society as a whole.[68]

Those friendships which rest upon pleasure or utility are to be recognized conventionally as friendship. These types of friendships may evolve into virtuous friendships over time if the individuals continue to grow and mature in wisdom. However, the highest form of friendship is based on the deep concern and love for the other individual and not on self-indulgence or on an immature or imbalanced neediness.[69]

Aristotle elaborates further on the type of character one should seek in finding and establishing virtuous friendships, suggesting that the only basis for *philia* is essentially objective. The traits one should look for in a friend include those who share our dispositions, who bear no grudges, who seek what we do, who are temperate and just, and who admire us appropriately just as we admire them. *Philia* cannot emanate from those who are quarrelsome, gossips, aggressive in manner and personality, or who are unjust, for example.[70]

The best moral character, according to Aristotle, may produce the best kind of friendship, and the highest form of *philia* love. In fact, being of good character worthy of *philia* is the theme of Aristotle's *Nicomachaen Ethics*. The most rational man is the one who would be the happiest and therefore the one most capable of the best form of friendship, which between two "who are good and alike in virtue" is rare. Love between such equals—Aristotle's rational and happy men—would be perfect friendship.[71]

From a modern perspective, one might consider this deepest form of virtuous friendship as consisting of only one or two friends whom we allow into our most intimate "circle of trust," while all others are simply companions on the journey. Friendships of a lesser quality may be based instead on the pleasure or utility that is derived from another's company. For example, a business friendship is based on utility, on mutual reciprocity of similar business interests. Once the business is at an end, the friendship often dissolves.

Similarly, those acquaintances based primarily upon the pleasure that is derived from each other's company, or which flow from satisfying one's desire for good humor or affirmation, would not be considered virtuous *philia* love by Aristotle. For example, men who enjoy watching baseball games or other sporting events together without a deeper bond, or simply working out at the gym together, would not fit within Aristotle's definition of a virtuous friendship. Moreover, a "hook-up" with another person, designed simply to achieve physical pleasure, would not fit within the definition of *philia* love.

Aristotle suggests that the first condition for the highest form of Aristotelian love is that a man loves himself. Without a balanced ego, a man cannot extend sympathy and affection to others. Instead, he is likely to be narcissistic, clinging to others, seeking to find in them the security and validation he cannot find within himself.

Healthy self-love is not hedonistic, since it does not depend on the pursuit of immediate pleasures or seek adulation. The ability to honor one's self is instead a reflection of a man's noble pursuit of virtuous character, which culminates in a balanced, reflective life. Friendship is the core part of such a virtuous life, according to Aristotle, "since [the virtuous man's] purpose is to contemplate worthy actions ... to live pleasantly ... sharing in discussion and thought" as is appropriate for him and his friend.[72]

Reciprocity, although not necessarily equal, is another condition of Aristotelian love and friendship.[73] A true friend must be willing to mutually give and receive love.

Socrates' writings and conversations further enrich Greek ethics on the topic of friendships. Socrates also adopted the term *philia* to differentiate the love between friends, from *eros*, the love between husband and wife. Socrates believed that the best of all possessions was a sincere and good friend. Yet, he wrote, most people are more careless with their friends than they are with their servants or physical possessions. A good friend, according to Socrates, is one who is loyal and helpful in watching one's private fortune and public career, in contributing, rescuing from trouble, sharing expenses, defending one's position, celebrating success, and helping a friend up when his companion falls.[74]

Socrates was not afraid to put someone on the spot so that he might recall the obligations of one's friendship. Once when his companion Antisthenes had been neglecting his poverty-stricken friend, Socrates asked him in the presence of his friend what dollar value Antisthenes placed on his friendship. Such a conversation was obviously designed to stir the man into action on behalf of his friend.

Socrates provided a list of moral qualities to use as a test for the soundness of one's friendships. According to Socrates, if one is the slave of eating and drinking, lust, sleep, or idleness, he cannot do what he should for himself or for his friend. The spendthrift or the stingy and selfish business person offers little in the way of friendship. The quarrelsome person makes too many enemies. The one who receives favors without giving anything in return does not deserve the gift of friendship. Socrates wrote:

> "We shall look for one who controls his indulgence in the pleasures of the body, who is truly hospitable and fair in his dealings and eager to do as much for his benefactors as he receives from them, so that he is worth knowing."[75]

To test these qualities, Socrates recommended that one look at the person's works to see if they are fruitful and good. This method of assessing character is similar to how one might judge the works of a sculptor or examine how a farmer treats his animals.[76]

In addition to Socrates, Plato also wrote extensively on the topic of friendships. For Plato, the best and highest form of love is to direct one's mind to the love of divinity. In Plato's view, the purpose of friendship is solely to inspire the mind and the soul of each man to direct his attention to spiritual things alone.[77]

In his dialogues, Plato clearly regards sexual contact between friends and lovers as a degraded and wasteful form of erotic expression. Because the true goal of love is to capture real beauty through what Plato calls "beauty itself," unless individuals channel their power of love into "higher pursuits," they are likely to be frustrated and unfulfilled.[78] From this ethical backdrop came the term *platonic relationships*, defined as those which are chaste and nonsexual, which transcend physical desire and tend toward the spiritual or ideal.[79]

The Christian tradition is deeply rooted in the classical Greek and Roman foundation regarding the virtue of friendship. Early Christian writers incorporated much of classic thought on the topic. They insisted that the virtue of friendship is not only an appropriate but also a necessary means toward spiritual growth and enlightenment.

Steeped in the model of Jesus' life, the Christian tradition has historically emphasized the importance of friendship as a pathway toward the fullness of life, particularly as depicted in the gospel of John. According to Paul O'Callaghan, in his book *The Feast of Friendship*, one of the key messages of the gospel of John is the presentation of Jesus as friend.[80] Jesus is found to have unique friendships with both Lazarus and John. For example, John is often called the Beloved, the one whom Jesus loved.[81] Additionally, Jesus' strong emotional response to the death of Lazarus caused the Jews to remark, "See how he loved him."[82]

After Jesus' death, many Christian patriarchs followed Christ's practice in not only writing about but also deeply experiencing the gift of their own human friendships. Perhaps the best known and most influential Christian writer on the topic of friendships was Aelred of Rievaulx with his treatise *Spiritual Friendships*.[83] His writings, and those of many other church fathers, have developed a "theology of friendship", which recent authors such as Paul O'Callaghan and Dan Steiger suggest needs to be dusted off and rekindled.[84]

Aelred was a monk and the abbot of the great English Cistercian abbey of Rievaulx from 1147 to 1167. During his abbacy, he built Rievaulx into a place of spiritual welcome and prosperity, desiring to make it "a mother of mercy" to those in need.

In his three-book Ciceronian-style dialogue, Aelred defined human friendship as sacramental. Friendships arise out of God's creative power and God's desire to place men in divine relationship with him and with other human beings. Human friendships are linked with and to Christ. They are the culmination of God's love for humanity. For Aelred, the scriptural passage "God is love" is easily interpreted to mean "God is friendship," an ideal to which all human friendships should aspire.[85]

Drawing significantly from the writings of Cicero's *De Amicitia*, Aelred viewed the Greek virtue of friendship through a Christian lens, proposing that friendship is not simply a social grace or ethical virtue, as suggested by Cicero, but rather a necessary means to spiritual perfection.[86] According to Aelred, friendship springs from God. Therefore, it is a natural desire for humans to want to share their lives with others as committed friends.

For Aelred, there is no conflict between love of our friends and the love of God, since all love is one, with its source in God. In fact, Aelred writes that if we are to truly love God, we must form loving friendships with others whose foundation is in the love of God so that we can carry out God's desire that we love our neighbor as ourselves.[87]

According to Aelred, men cannot be truly happy in this world without committed friendships.[88] His identification of spiritual friendship with the perfect love of God allowed Aelred to make the bold statement that "God is friendship."[89] For Aelred, the existence of a true spiritual friendship was a sign and symbol of the divine life of the Trinity.

Spiritual friendships, as defined by Aelred, are "those relationships which lead men further on the path toward God." This type of friendship "begins in Christ, is preserved according to the Spirit of Christ ... and its end and fruition are Christ."[90] Like the Holy Trinity, spiritual friends remain distinct individuals who are formed by and become one in God. God is the third person in the spiritual friendship who unites the friends' hearts as they move deeper inward on the God-path. According to Aelred, "And thus, friend cleaving to a friend in the spirit of Christ, is made with Christ but one heart and one soul, and so mounting aloft through degrees of love to friendship with Christ, he is made one spirit with him in one kiss."[91]

Aelred is careful to point out, just as Cicero did, that not all friendships are virtuous. According to Aelred, there are three kinds of friendships, only one of which can be called a spiritual friendship.

The first Aelred calls a "carnal friendship," which springs from mutual harmony in vice. The second form he calls a "worldly friendship," which is kindled by the hope of gain. The third, a "spiritual friendship," is "cemented by similarity of life, morals, and pursuits among the just."[92] It is for spiritual friendships that Aelred suggests all men must aspire to if they wish to find wholeness.

The four qualities that Aelred believes must be tested in a friend before one can trust himself to the friendship and discern whether it is a spiritual friendship or not are loyalty, right intention, discretion, and patience.[93]

Loyalty, according to Aelred, is that character in a man that causes him to be a true companion in all things—good or bad. A truly loyal friend "sees nothing in his friend but his heart."[94]

Right intention means that one expects nothing from the friendship except God and the other friend's natural goodness.

Discretion requires a sense of discernment, an ability to understand through their prayer and connection with God what one must do or seek for their friend in any given situation. The wisdom arising out of such discretion allows a friend to understand what sufferings are to be endured for and with one's friend, what should be encouraged in one's friend, and, by knowing deeply what faults one's friend possesses, pointing out what must be corrected in one's friend in the right manner, time, and place.

With the virtue of patience, a friend is not to be offended when rebuked by his friend. Patience creates endurance and the willingness to bear "every adversity for the sake of his friend."[95]

These four qualities of spiritual friendship, according to Aelred, must be carefully tested over time between those who are considering admitting each other into friendship, since the relationship between two friends, if from God, will indeed be transformative for both. He describes such a friendship with these words:

> For since your friend is the companion of your soul, to whose spirit you join and attach yours, and so associate yourself that you wish to become one instead of two, since he is one to whom you entrust yourself as to another self, from whom you hide nothing, from whom you fear nothing, you should, in the first place, surely choose one who is considered fitted for all this. Then he is to be tried, and so finally admitted. For friendship should be stable and manifest a certain likeness to eternity, persevering always in affection.[96]

If all four of these qualities are present in a friendship, Aelred writes, then one can consider the friendship is truly a gift from God given to each of the friends so they might grow in virtue, love, and wholeness. The two friends then become one in Christ and are transformed by their mutual love and respect for each other into the image of Christ.[97]

Aelred suggests that just as Christ had two spiritual friends, John and Peter, who were closer to him than any of the other disciples, each man should follow Christ's model and strive to have one or two close friends whom he considers "spiritual friends."[98] All other friends, who may very well be good for one's soul, would not be considered spiritual friends, but rather simply good comrades. Having two or more of these deeper friendships promotes and maintains a healthy relationship among the spiritual friends by avoiding an unhealthy exclusivity, which could move the friendship into a place of codependency or even to a sexualized relationship.[99]

In addition to the writings of Aelred of Rievaulx, the fathers of the Christian church, including Saints Basil, Gregory the Theologian, Anselm, Augustine, Jerome, and John Cassian, wrote extensively about the virtue of spiritual friendships. They embraced the classic tradition of friendship espoused by Aristotle and Cicero. However, their focus came through a Christian lens. The Greco-Roman tradition upon which the church fathers rooted their treatises described these key elements of a virtuous friendship as follows:

> A fundamental belief in reciprocity as a *sine quo non* of friendship, a high degree of intimacy between two or at most a few persons which made it possible to think of a friend as a second self; the idea that a friend ought to possess some reason for being loved, which in the case of good men would be their virtue, and that friends should share material things and have interests in common.[100]

The Fathers' writings formed the foundation for a "Theology of Friendship."[101] Classical themes such as one's friend as a second self, the recognition of virtue in the other, the mutuality of interests, and the sharing of things in common echo throughout the distinctly Christian voice of the fathers.[102]

For example, Gregory the Theologian wrote the following concerning his friendship with Basil the Great during the early years of their friendship:

> We had all things in common, and a single soul, as it was, bound together in two distinct bodies. But above all it was God, of course, and a mutual desire for higher things, that drew us to each other. As a result, we reached such a pitch of confidence

that we revealed the depths of our hearts, becoming ever more united in our yearnings. There is no such solid bond of union as thinking the same thoughts.[103]

The Christian theology of friendship added one important dimension to the classical view of friendships with the core belief that "the origin of the friendship is in God and its orientation is toward the pursuit of God."[104] Moreover, the Christian fathers were not writing out of an abstract theological concept of friendship, but rather from their own experiences of rich and deep friendships themselves.[105]

One of the major questions that arose out of the fathers' experiences was whether it was appropriate for a Christian to have friendships that were termed "particular and preferential." This issue emerged from the fact that many of the church fathers lived in monastic communities. The concern in such communities was that a preferential friendship, i.e., one in which a man gives special love and attention to another friend above others, would either be a potential temptation to sexual immorality or would destroy common harmony in the community by fostering unequal affection among the members of the monastery.[106] While there were differing opinions about whether particular friendships were appropriate inside the monastic community, the concern was not shared by those outside of the monastery.

John Cassian used the example of Jesus' special love for the apostle John as a model for Christian friendship to support the appropriateness of preferential friendships in the Christian tradition.[107] Summarizing the fourth-century perspective on Christian friendship, Carolinne White captures Cassian's experience and writings as follows:

> This deep affection for one particular disciple did not imply that Jesus' love for the other disciples was lukewarm, but that he felt superabundant love for John because of John's chastity and purity. Far from condemning such special, partial feelings [Cassian] regards them as more sublime, for to him they imply the perfection of virtue and great love.[108]

Gregory the Theologian defended his special loyalty and devotion for his friend Nicoboulous by pointing to God's unique relationship with the favored nation of Israel.[109] For Gregory, friendship was the highest value one could seek in life. He wrote, "If anyone were to ask me, 'What is the best thing in life?' I would answer, 'Friends.'"[110]

According to Gregory and many other church fathers, God draws men together as friends as a manifestation of unfolding divine destiny. The purpose of those friendships is to point each other toward God. Hence, like Jonathan and David, God knits the hearts of friends together with divine grace.[111]

During the 1800 and 1900s, the concept of spiritual friendships continued, but in a more secular fashion. Daniel Webster referred to deep male friendships as a romantic friendship. These unique relationships, according to Webster, were based on a sharing of innermost thoughts and secret emotions.[112]

Webster's journals and correspondence are filled with stories about his special friendships with several men, especially his intense friendship with James Hervey Bingham. These relationships, he described, contributed immensely to his well-being. Webster called his best friend Bingham "the partner of my joys, griefs, and affections, the only participator of my most secret thoughts."[113] According to Webster, from among the pool of one's casual companions that men enjoy throughout their life, a man needs to choose several special friends who share a congenial spirit and develop closer ties with them.

A similar form of bosom friendship is found in the relationship between James Blake and Wyck Vanderhoef. The two met in 1848, during their early twenties. As their friendship blossomed, Blake exulted, writing in his diary, "I have found a *friend!* one upon whom I can repose every trust, and when in trouble and affliction can seek relief."[114] Having found such a friend in Wyck, Blake wrote what a "beautiful thing" it was to "retire from the cold selfish arms of the world, and receive the pure embrace of friendship."[115]

According to the writings from this period, it was clear that many of these friendships included a physical bond that involved touching and holding each other in a nonsexual fashion. In fact, it was common in the culture of the nineteenth century for men to sleep together side by side and even hold each other. Blake wrote in his diary, reflecting on his visit with his friend Wyck, "We retired early and in each other's arms did friendship sink peacefully to sleep."[116] It was common for Blake, as well as for other men in deep friendships, to not only share a friend's bed but share embraces there as well.[117]

The evidence of similar types of caring friendships between men can be readily found in the diaries and correspondence of many other men during this era. This special form of friendship, according to Anthony Rotundo, "evoked no apologies and elicited no condemnation; apparently, it was accepted without question among middle-class male youth."[118] It was a "normal, common form of behavior" during this era.[119]

Romantic friendships between two men during the nineteenth century thus were physical, but not sexual, according to historians. Sex was linked to reproduction, and reproduction was not possible between two men. Therefore, the close relationship was not interpreted as being sexual in nature.[120] As a result, both men and women of this era could write of affectionate desire for a person of the same gender without causing any concern.[121]

This acceptance of the romantic nature of male friendships seems to be based in part on the fact that there were no words for or concept of homosexuality. Instead, if homosexuality was even thought about, it was thought of only in terms of a particular sexual act, such as engaging in anal or oral genital contact, not as an identity or a particular characteristic.[122] In fact, sleeping in the same bed with another man or exchanging a kiss on the cheek or an embrace were viewed as gestures of strong affection and affirmation, not as an act of sexual expression, according to Rotundo.[123]

This type of deep affection between men was viewed by nineteenth-century culture as socially akin to the type of chivalry, comradeship, and heroism affirmed in ancient Greece and in medieval Europe as a pathway to growing male strength and virtue.[124] These male-male friendships ranged from casual to intimate to romantic. The physical component varied, but often clearly included hugs, kisses, and sleeping together. Men recognized the range of acceptable physical closeness between men and drew their own boundaries based on personality and cultural heritage.[125] In short, the physical expression of affection, be it embracing or sharing a bed, carried no negative stigma for men in the nineteenth century. Instead, these deep male friendships, along with the physical closeness which accompanied them, were culturally supported and affirmed.[126]

A dramatic shift, however, occurred at the turn of the nineteenth century. Historians reflect that by the end of that century, the concept of romantic male friendships became an artifact. This death knell for deep male friendships continues in today's Western culture.

According to sociology professor Peter Nardi, contemporary society has over time constructed a set of social meanings and prohibitions against homosexuality to such an extreme degree that even ordinary touches among men and certainly the idea of two men sleeping in the same bed together are often interpreted in homosexual terms. This has resulted in isolating modern men from each other due to the fear of social stigma.[127] In fact, studies of friendship today consistently show that close friendship is "rarely" experienced by men in our Western culture.[128]

One wonders why twentieth-century culture became an anomaly in its view of male friendships both in Western culture and in the church despite: (a) the rich historical heritage from classical philosophy; and (b) Christian theological tradition supporting the importance of male friendships as pathways toward virtue and spiritual growth.

Put simply, to what or to whom do we attribute the loss of legitimate male friendship and the decline of men? We now turn our attention to the answer.

Chapter 4
Where Did All My Friends Go?

A number of factors have influenced the pendulum shift away from the virtue of spiritual friendships toward the resulting isolationism of men. Three key developments stand out as the primary causes for this dramatic decline in close male friendships during the twentieth century:

1. *Legalism*—The spirit of legalism which grew out of the Reformation and the Counter-Reformation.
2. *Collapse of* philia *love into eros*—The loss of *philia* love as a framework for understanding deep male connection as a form of legitimate nonsexual love.
3. *The feminization of men*—The development of the soft male with the resulting loss of male strength as an important virtue.[129]

A closer examination of each of these factors will help pinpoint their roots and highlight their historical impact.

Legalism

The hysteria within the church growing out of the Reformation and the Counter-Reformation shaped a distrust of male friendships which were deemed "particular." As the church sought to eliminate many of the problems for which it had fallen under attack, including abuse of clerical power and questionable relationships between some men living in monastic communities, the hierarchy moved into a period of strict legalism. During the late 1800s and early 1900s, Catholic church officials established severe rules and restrictions designed to prevent the type of behavior which had become troublesome within its institutions.

In order to address the abuse of power that had occurred among ordained clergy and those living in monastic communities, physical closeness between men was banned in most cloistered communities.[130] Suddenly, the most ordinary of personal contacts were viewed with deep suspicion.[131] This strict bar against any physical closeness between men spilled over from the church's walls into the pews as the clergy sought to impose similar types of restrictions on the lay community to whom they preached.[132]

The collapse of philia love into eros

During the late 1800s and into the early 1900s, Sigmund Freud revolutionized the study and practice of psychology, postulating that sexual drives were the primary motivational forces of human life. Freud contended that every human relationship is rooted in one's basic sexual needs and desires (libido, or eros).

The impact of his psychosexual theories, which gained broad acceptance and appeal, resulted in society soon sexualizing what other generations had seen as purely platonic friendships. As a result, *philia* love as a classic virtue (which had for centuries been deemed a normal healthy part of the masculine personality) collapsed into eros. This development led to an eventual abandonment of the Greco-Roman ideal of *philia* love.

Labels such as "congenital inversion" and "perversion" replaced the traditional term of *philia* love to describe men's desires for deep connection with other men.[133] As a result, the concept of homosexuality, which had traditionally been viewed and applied as a term to describe a specific sexual act between the genitals of two individuals of the same gender, broadened into an identity, or personality. Freud's broad brush painting all human behaviors as arising out of one's sexual needs eliminated the possibility that *philia* love could be rooted in something other than eros.[134]

Father Paul O'Callaghan, in his book *The Feast of Friendship*, suggests that the loss of the theology of friendship has been directly caused by our modern culture confusing *philia* love with eros. This loss is the result of having sexualized all relationships and physical desires. In other words, we have left no room in our culture for a nonsexual *philia* relationship between men.

Although the boundary between the two types of love is thin at times, they are very distinct. And, says O'Callaghan, it is certainly possible to love another person of the same gender intensely as a friend without a sexual connotation. In short, according to O'Callaghan, our Freudian preoccupation with sex is due in part to the fact that "our culture has forgotten the nature of philia and does not make allowance for its expression."[135] This, he believes, has resulted in giving men only two choices: live without deep male connections or be chastised for being suspected of being homosexual. There is no room left for anything in between.[136]

The feminization of men

A third cause of the loss of deep male friendships over the last century is the gradual shift, both in our culture and in the church, from a patriarchal toward a more matriarchal society. This shift has led to the feminization of men, known by the metaphor the "soft male."

As pointed out by Robert Bly in *Iron John*, the advancement and empowerment of women through the women's movement have indeed been a good development for women and society.[137] In broad cultural terms, there is a historical cycle of masculine/feminine rise and decline which exists throughout the course of time. According to Bly, we are presently experiencing a "transition from centuries of static masculinity (patriarchy) to dynamic femininity (feminism)."[138]

This rising tide, which has the positive effect of promoting equilibrium between men and women in society and in the church, also has its shadow side. This shadow side places men in the difficult, never-before-experienced climate in which they must live, work, and grow. Masculinity, Bly believes, is under attack. That attack is not just on the negative qualities; the positive virtues of strength, courage, and passion have become suspect.[139]

The fallout from the promotion of female equality has resulted in a deep, almost exclusive focus on male-female friendships and a deep suspicion of intense emotional friendships between men.[140] At its extreme, the movement from a patriarchal toward a matriarchal society has resulted in a form of misandry—the hatred of men, known simply as "male-bashing."[141] According to Bly, "In recent decades the separatist wing of the feminist movement, in a justified fear of brutality, has labored to breed fierceness out of men."[142]

The above three factors have resulted in a major shift toward rebalancing humanity in terms of the mutuality between men and women. However, the pendulum for the past decade has shifted away from the unhealthy oppression of women toward, unfortunately, the unhealthy oppression of men.[143] The fallout from this dramatic shift is the increasing isolationism being experienced by men.

Since the 1980s, with the advent of the men's movement, however, there has been a counterbalancing emerging from this cultural shift in the form of the growing desire among men to better understand and redefine their own masculinity. This rebalancing is not a return to patriarchy, but rather the emergence of a more authentic masculinity. According to Bly, now more than ever, men are being invited to do the inner spiritual work necessary to understand what it means to be a man and to recapture the male spirit that makes men unique and valuable in their distinct gifts as men.[144] Bly explains it this way:

> Masculinity must not be taken for granted; it is amazingly fragile and subject to failure and ridicule. It is surprisingly ephemeral, and ever in need of renewal and reassertion. It is an endangered resource. For all its blessings and curses, masculinity is no better—and no worse—than femininity; it is one-half of what it means to be human. So if we do not treasure masculinity, we cannot be said to love humanity. And if we do not know the masculine voice and tone, its values and qualities, its metaphors and archetypes, we cannot begin to understand God.[145]

According to Bly, men are realizing that this inner journey is not a solo path. It requires other men to walk alongside them to blow the dust from one's eyes and encourage each other along the way. Like the rich young man standing in front of Christ, men today also stand at a crossroads, collectively and individually, asking the question, "Good teacher, what must I do to gain the fullness of life?" The answer remains consistent throughout the ages, "Come follow me."

Unlike the rich young man, however, this time not all men are turning away and going back to their old way of life. The discontent is too sharp. The isolationism is too painful. The resolve that men were made for more than this is simply too strong.

In light of this new emerging source of male energy and desire, the question presents itself, "How can men and pastoral counselors grip this new vision of wholeness? How can they find the tools they need, the compasses, guides, and companions, to take the fork in the road and move forward into a deeper more authentic way of living?"

The answer, in part, is found in breaking the man code (the unwritten rules which govern how men must interact with each other), so that men can find the wholeness they seek.

Chapter 5
Breaking the Man Code to Become a Man

Ask a man to tell you what the man code is, and you're likely to garner a snicker in reply. The snicker suggests at least two things: that there are a number of unwritten rules which impose a series of cultural constraints on how men are supposed to interact with each other (and this man knows at least some of them) and he knows it's a violation of the man code to talk seriously about these rules since one of the man code rules is the conspiracy of silence surrounding them.

The man code (also referred to as the "man rules") is the unwritten societal code of conduct to which a man's man subscribes, lest he appear unmanly. The man rules require men to *act* as if they don't care about anything or anyone and may even lead them to *believe* they don't care. The rules restrict men's conversations with other men to the safe subjects of work, cars, home improvements, women, and sports.[146]

The man rules require men to avoid any subject that would allow one man to enter into the inner world of another man and suggest a man is weak or in need of help.

These cultural constraints directly hinder the level of male bonding, since one of the unwritten rules men fear breaking, lest they lose their masculine stature, is that if you get too close to another man, you are clearly gay. According to Peter Nardi's research on the topic of male friendships and masculinity, homophobia has clearly limited the discussion of loving male relationships and led to the denial by men of the real importance of their friendships with other men.[147]

The open expression of emotion and affection by men toward other men in today's culture is thought to be characteristic only of homosexuals. Hence, men in our modern society are raised with a mixed message: "Strive for healthy, emotionally intimate friendships, but be careful—if you appear too intimate with another man, you might be negatively labeled homosexual."[148] Therefore, to be masculine in today's culture requires men to distance themselves from any behavior that might indicate homosexuality, including emotionally close friendships with other men.[149]

These cultural restrictions on men being intimate with other men has resulted in the development of a "covert intimacy," according to Michael Messner. This covert intimacy springs out of the cultural idol worship of male sports figures in our modern society. It allows men, through the sports subculture, to share a safe, watered-down form of indirect intimacy.

The sports-based friendship is typically task-oriented by nature, since it involves watching or playing an athletic event together. However, once the game is over, other than sharing game statistics, the purpose of the friendship has been accomplished and there is no room for deeper connection between the two men.[150] As a result, the friendship typically does not extend beyond the game. There is little, if any, opportunity for men to share a deeper intellectual, emotional, or spiritual connection. Unfortunately, this type of watered-down, sports-based friendship has become the cultural norm for men.

Intimacy, Messner defines as "one's ability to share their inner life with another person." Covert intimacy is characterized by "doing together," rather than by "being together," through mutual talk about each other's inner lives.[151]

The problem with shallow sports-based friendships is that while these friendships are certainly very valuable and an important part of men's socialization, they fail miserably in helping men gain and pass on the inner wisdom and spiritual growth they need to become healthy men, husbands, fathers, and mentors to other men. In other words, friendships which are based primarily on watching or engaging in sports tend to be emotionally impoverished.

In fact, this type of covert intimacy is often detrimental to men, since it requires men to wear artificial masks of perceived success and power to protect themselves from each other.[152] It leads to men becoming performance-based, defined not by their integrity and compassion, but by their outward success or perceived success.

This form of masquerading is evidenced by the typical response of "Fine" when a man is asked by another man, "How are you doing?" On its surface, the response suggests everything is terrific. However, such a response often masks the fact that one's life is out of control.[153]

The sports-friendship model of male bonding without intimacy reinforces the fifties type of man—the one who is empty and shallow and doesn't understand why. Such limited friendships do little to help men take the inner journey of the deep male, fail to initiate other men into true manhood, and offer few opportunities for mentoring and passing down the wisdom of older men. Moreover, this type of friendship stands in stark contrast to the image of masculinity modeled by Jesus, who was both strong and powerful as a man, yet willing to share deep compassion with and for his disciples.[154]

In short, the current model of covert intimacy places modern men in a quandary—having to define one's masculinity through the lens of sports or outward achievements, while distancing oneself from any type of intimate behavior with other men in order to avoid being labeled homosexual.

This quandary is the one in which Luke, whose case study was discussed earlier, found himself: wanting deep male connection, but boxed in by society's man rules which would label him gay if he attempted to use unconventional means to find the connection he needed.

Luke had to break the man rules to find his own masculinity. Railing against these culturally imposed rules, Luke became an unintentional pioneer. He got in touch with his inner self. He became vulnerable. He willingly shared his heart with other men. By allowing his legitimate needs for intellectual, emotional, spiritual, and physical connection with other men to be met in a nonsexual way, he found healing and strength through the masculine validation he received from another man. Most importantly, he demanded a loving God explain to him why he felt the way he did. In response, grace blazed a new path for Luke and gave him the wisdom to follow that path.

Luke's determination empowered him to refuse to settle for either meaningless male friendships suffocated with endless sports talk or to reduce his desires to a hapless search for sexual connection with other men. In the end, Luke was able to discover his heart's truest desire: deep meaningful relationships with other men on all four levels: intellectual, emotional, physical, and spiritual.

It took Luke many years of Don Quixote–like searching and lots of hard inner work to get to a place of deeper peace. But unlike the rich young man who walked away from wholeness, Luke battled on. He surrendered to the invitation of his heart and found God's strength through his own weakness. Waiting for him on the other side of this inner, deep male journey, he found what he was looking for: freedom.

Perhaps Luke's inner journey is the same journey every man wanting to find freedom and wholeness must take—an inner journey that requires the courage to break the man rules our culture imposes on men today so that men can be free to ask themselves the simple, yet pivotal question, "What do I really want?"

CHAPTER 6
WHAT DO MEN REALLY WANT?
DEEP MALE CONNECTION

This personal ad was posted recently in the platonic section of a local Craig's List website under "Men Seeking Men":

> I am learning to name these days that what many men, including myself, are looking for is what used to be called "spiritual friendships"—that is, friendships among 2-3 good buddies who share their intellectual, emotional, spiritual and physical selves. I am interested in developing these kinds of friendships with a couple of good buddies who are like-minded. I am happily married, in good shape, love to work out 3x per week, run, hike, fish, camp, read, teach, mentor, write and learn about spirituality. I also love to give and receive rub downs from good buddies. If you are in good shape and are looking for a similar type of long term friendship, shoot me an email and your pic and let's see if we can connect and share the journey as great friends.

This ad exemplifies the growing restlessness within men to articulate and satisfy their natural need for deep male connection. It also suggests that men are becoming more open and willing to pursue authentic relationships with other men as they gain the courage to cast aside the fear of being labeled gay, weird, or a crackpot. Possibly C. S. Lewis's prophetic words in his 1960 book *The Four Loves*, buried quietly within his chapter on male-to-male love, are gradually becoming a reality:

> It has actually become necessary in our time to rebut the theory that every firm and serious friendship is homosexual.[155]

When the author of the above Craig's List post was interviewed as part of the research for this book, this question was posed to him: "What are you looking for?" His response was revealing:

I am looking for a buddy. Someone who is willing to love me as a man. Not in a sexual way, but in a way that is real and authentic and enhances my marriage with my wife and my role as a father. A guy that I can say anything to and he won't reject me. A guy who will help me on my up and down walk on the God-path. A buddy who has my back. Who can mirror for me who I am, who I am not and who I am becoming. Someone that is willing to strip away all the masks us guys wear with each other and be real with me so I can be real with him and with myself. A buddy I can give and receive love with—another kind of love—different than the love I have for my wife.

Other Craig's List personal ads suggest many men desire what this man is looking for: deep authentic male connection. Men simply haven't been able to articulate it. Sadly, society has failed to give men room to express this form of nonsexual love, much less allow them to celebrate their unique gifts of masculinity.[156]

Despite the failure of society to give men the freedom to find and enjoy rich male friendships, the literature over the last decade on men's issues consistently repeats a common theme: men are created to connect deeply and authentically with other men. Scripture puts it simply: iron sharpens iron.[157] If men don't connect deeply with other men, they come out sideways and often quickly fall into unhealthy behaviors and attitudes which are harmful to themselves, to their spouses, and to their families.

The cost of this unhealthy state of drifting manhood has devastated our society as a whole. Its brokenness spills out into the streets of society and rears its head in the form of drug and pornography addiction, divorce, single-parent homes, gang warfare, and fatherless and abused children which, for far too long, has been the status quo.[158]

Jared Feria and Lance Hastings, a son-in-law and father-in-law men's ministry team, report that after more than ten years of working with men and dealing with their own masculine struggles, what they and most men want, is what they describe as "a friend-who-sticks-closer-than-a-brother" kind of love.[159] Quoting Stu Weber from his book *Locking Arms*,[160] Hastings and Feria write:

What Do Men Really Want?
Deep Male Connection

Deep down at the core, every many needs a friend. Deep down at the core, every man needs a brother to lock arms with. Down deep at the core, every many needs a soul mate.[161]

If Scripture, current men's literature, C. S. Lewis, Hastings, Feria, and Weber are all accurate in describing what men need and want in the form of legitimate male connection, then two questions naturally arise:

What efforts have been made to help men connect deeply with each other?

What additional steps can be undertaken to foster such continued growth in men?

What efforts have been made to help men connect deeply with each other?

Tom McGrath in the 2008 U.S. Catholic magazine article titled *Is Men's Spirituality Out of the Woods?*[162] reports that just as a handful of pioneer women during the women's movement of the 1960s had to discover their inner voice and power by examining what true womanhood meant for them and for society, men today are being invited to engage in similar "men's work." This men's work empowers men to walk alongside each other on the spiritual journey and provides the opportunity for men to connect with their own and each other's hearts.

Men's work, according to McGrath, is "a process that allows men to examine their inner wounds; reclaim the power, passion and energy that flows from their values; helps them discover their mission and calling; and gives them structures to live in a deeper way."[163] Men's work moves men from self-sufficiency—with the constant suspicion that we're not good enough—to the heart of spiritual growth, which is vulnerability and reliance on God [and other men]."[164]

The men's work that McGrath describes is similar to the deep male Robert Bly encourages men to grow toward in his groundbreaking book *Iron John*, the book which launched the secular men's movement into popular view in the 1990s. McGrath believes this inner work is initiated in our culture by the Holy Spirit and fostered in several ways. Some of the more common ways experienced over the last decade include the following:

The round 'em up and give 'em a charge approach
This approach, most evident in the Promise Keeper's model, is common in many churches. It entails inviting men to a specific round-up event where men's roles in the family and the world are examined and men are given clear challenges on how to live a good and decent life. Men at these events are charged up and given a noble task to pursue.[165]

While this model meets men's immediate needs for respect and a call to arms,[166] it often results in the same letdown the disciples experienced after the Transfiguration. There at the top of the mountain with Jesus, Moses, and Elijah, the disciples encountered an amazing out-pouring of grace and clarity, but they did not want to come down from the mountain, fearing they would quickly lose the peace and power they had experienced. Similarly, when men come down from the "mountaintop experience" of a weekend Promise Keepers type of event, they often report a deep letdown as they return to the drudgery of daily life, causing a dashing of hopes and expectations as they once again travel alone on their day-to-day paths.

The process of initiation
The initiation process grows out of the experience Jesus had during his forty days in the desert. It creates an experience where men remove themselves from their comfortable world, go out into the wilderness, and face their demons. When a ritual structure is placed around the experience, it becomes a process of initiation.

This process is part of an almost universally practiced rite that many cultures have used for centuries by which men learn to "commit their power to the common good."[167] Although our American culture has lost much of the sense of this rite of initiation for men, there are more and more men's groups over the last decade that are offering retreat experiences to initiate men into mature male spirituality. One example of this type of initiation retreat is the Men's Rites of Passage retreat designed and offered by Richard Rohr.[168]

The funnel approach
The funnel approach of inviting men to go deeper in their masculinity involves staging a large men's event focused on transformation and then funneling men into smaller groups at the parish or local church level for ongoing growth and support. It has the advantage of giving men a place to continue to grow as they come down from the "mountaintop."

The follow-up offered by such groups holds the possibility of creating safe places where men can do their inner work in the company of other men committed to the spiritual journey. This approach has been further supported through the resources created by the U.S. Catholic Conference of Bishops known as the National Resource Center for Catholic Men.[169]

Men's Bible study groups, discussion or prayer groups
This has been the primary method that men have used to connect with each other and foster commitment to their spiritual growth. These groups usually involve meeting to share a meal, with a specific spiritual topic or book to be studied and discussed.

These types of groups create space for men to satisfy their needs for fellowship. However, they can often disband when the focus becomes too social. They can also limit the scope of men's inner work if the men in the group are not willing to move beyond the man rules and share their inner struggles with each other.

Men's group spiritual direction
This method of gatherings for men rises out of the Quaker and Christian contemplative models of community meetings. It has been adopted and refined by several spiritual life centers using a *lectio divina* style of invoking and experiencing the presence of the Holy Spirit through gentle intercessory prayer.

In these meetings, men create a closed group of typically five to seven men who agree to meet regularly, usually once a month for six months. The meeting consists of one man at a time, called the presenter, who shares with the group out loud, without interruption, for ten to twenty minutes about a current issue in his life through the lens of his relationship with God.

The group then holds the person in silent prayer and listens for a word or words, images, or Scripture that God places on their heart for the presenter. The group then offers what was placed on their heart to the presenter for him to ponder and hold in his own prayer.

The process is repeated for each man until all have had an opportunity to share. This contemplative model of discernment is based in part on the work and writings of St. Ignatius, who encouraged men and women to experience God through their hearts and imaginations.[170]

What additional steps can be undertaken to foster continued growth in men?

Spiritual friendships

While there are many other growing efforts to encourage men to do their inner work in the company of other men, the above are the most common. One method, however, which has not received much attention, is spiritual friendships. Spiritual friendships possibly offer the most lasting form of deep male connection since they are richly personal and ongoing. Spiritual friendships, however, violate the man code, since they involve moving closer to another man and developing a connection with him on a deeper, heart-to-heart level.

We stand at a crossroads in the area of men's relationships with each other. The current path offers men only two choices for male connection: isolationism or sexual expression. A third more unchartered path offers men the opportunity to develop and explore a richer more authentic relationship with other men through spiritual friendships.[171]

The spiritual friendship trail being blazed by men is a middle path. It offers a natural way for men to connect with each other intellectually, emotionally, physically, and spiritually. It also creates space for transformation through the development of deep male relationships men are hard-wired by God to enjoy. This middle path may have been the trail the rich young man was invited by Christ to follow as he stood face-to-face with Jesus and asked how he might find wholeness.

Forging this new path, however, requires trailblazers—men who are open to the restless stirring in their hearts and the movement of the Holy Spirit in their lives. It requires men who are unwilling to settle for the old, familiar—yet unsatisfying—answers society offers them; men who are willing to create the space in the midst of their loneliness for personal transformation to occur in the company of other men. The new trail also requires men and women who are willing to support these trailblazers in the process of self-awareness and integration.

To develop a deeper understanding of this emerging model of men's spirituality, let's explore the theology that forms the basis for these friendships. With the theological foundation in place, we can then examine questions about what these authentic male friendships look like and how men can find them.

Chapter 7
Spiritual Friendships
A Blast from the Past

Scripture instructs that iron sharpens iron.[172] In other words, men are designed for companionship with other men, to walk alongside each other, to sharpen the inner edges of their lives and personalities.[173] When there is no other iron with which to sharpen the edge of a sword, a sword soon becomes dull and useless. Sharpen that sword against a strong piece of steel, however, and the sword becomes a warrior's might. Similarly, when two men on the God-path engage each other in deep and honest friendship, the edges of their lives become stronger and more powerful. In such committed and trusting relationships, the two friends reflect back to each other the strengths and weaknesses of their character so they can both grow into mature and capable men.[174]

For Christians, Jesus is the embodiment of the Jewish ideal of "ish"—the fully mature and integrated man. Jesus' human life serves as a model for authentic masculinity. His relationships with his friends provide a blueprint for other men to pattern their male friendships.[175]

Several characteristics are evident in Jesus' life in connection with his male friends. First, the Son of Man freely chose (and perhaps needed) to surround himself with the love and companionship of other men willing to share their whole life with him. Second, Jesus experienced a deeper relationship with John, Peter, and Lazarus, much more profound than the relationship he had with his other companions. Third, Jesus gave and received strength, love, and encouragement from his closest male friends, which helped shape and form their lives and personalities.

From the above characteristics of Jesus' friendships, four pillars men might rely on to pattern and evaluate the integrity of their own male friendships become evident:

Jesus and his friends were deeply connected in four areas of their lives: emotionally, intellectually, physically, and spiritually.

Theirs was not an exclusive friendship, but rather a preferential friendship that Jesus shared with his friends. Because it was not mutually exclusive, the friendship enhanced and supported the other primary relationships in each man's life.

The friendship was formed naturally, there being an intuitive quality about it that suggests the friendship was initiated by and gifted to them from God.

The friends' primary focus was on helping each other walk closely with God in the day-to-day events of their lives.

These four pillars of spiritual friendship are important guidelines that can help men and the pastoral counselors who assist them define what men are seeking in the form of deep friendships and discern whether the friendships they discover are spiritual friendships or those of a more casual nature. These pillars help men do as Aelred of Rievaulx suggests they do: "Test the nature of the friendship to make sure it is of God."[176]

PILLAR ONE

Jesus and his friends were deeply connected in four areas of their lives: emotionally, intellectually, physically, and spiritually.

Jesus and John
Scripture often refers to Jesus' unique friendship with the "disciple whom [Jesus] loved dearly."[177] Surprisingly, this beloved disciple is never named. Tradition suggests that the beloved disciple was the apostle John. However, none of the Gospels confirm this. Some suggest that by leaving the beloved disciple nameless, he stands as an icon for the deeply devoted friendships Scripture invites all men to share with one or more close companions.[178] Surprisingly, the relationship between Jesus and John is only mentioned in the gospel of John, called by some the Gospel of friendship.[179]

The depth of Jesus' and John's friendship is demonstrated by their emotional and physical closeness. The physical presence between Jesus and John is depicted widely in paintings of the Last Supper.[180] John reclines upon Jesus' chest at the Last Supper.[181] He is the only disciple present at Jesus' crucifixion.[182] This physical bond signifies the deep connection of their hearts.[183]

Robert Bly suggests that men draw strength from each other through their physical presence. A substance much like food passes from one man to the other as a result of their physical closeness, much like the exchange of masculinity between a father and a son. An exchange takes place, he says, as if some substance passes directly to the cells of each man through the strength and healing presence of each other.[184]

With Bly's theory in mind, one wonders if Jesus needed the physical and emotional closeness of John reclining against him at the Last Supper so that he could absorb the masculine strength from John that he would need to carry out the excruciating task of the coming crucifixion.[185] Similarly, perhaps John needed the physical and emotional closeness of Jesus, the touch of his beard, the sound of his heartbeat to absorb the reality of his grief, to feel Jesus' strength, knowing he would soon no longer see his friend face-to-face nor walk with him shoulder-to-shoulder each day, as he had gotten accustomed to doing over the three years of their companionship.[186] The two men exchanged their strength in this moment at the Last Supper and on Calvary so that each received the inner power to endure the darkness that accompanied them in the last days of Jesus' earthly life. By knitting their hearts together emotionally, physically, and spiritually, God gifted Jesus and John with the masculinity they needed to carry out their tasks as men. As a result, they sharpened each other's iron through their presence with the vulnerability of their lives.

This reciprocal *philia* love between John and Jesus empowered John to walk alongside Jesus at a time when all others had abandoned him. John did not have the power to stop the violence inflicted on Jesus. However, out of John's inner strength, he did what men whose hearts are knit together in a bond of brotherly love do for each other: he stood near his friend with his abiding presence, from which both drew masculine strength.

John is the one to whom Jesus entrusted his mother at the end of his human life. Scripture notes that from that moment on, John took his best friend's mother into his home.[187] Jesus knew that above all other men, John had the heart for his mother that would most closely approximate his own because, as described by Paul O'Callaghan, the "sinews of his beloved's heart was inextricably intertwined with his" by virtue of their rich friendship.[188]

Intellectually, Jesus captivated John, along with the other disciples, through his parables. These moral stories about ordinary people and natural events engaged John's intellect, stretching him to experience the deeper wisdom Jesus was trying to help him understand. Through these stories, Jesus spoke directly to his friends' hearts, bypassing the resistance often imposed by the limitations of their minds.[189] Jesus used the metaphor, the story, the unexpected intellectual twist to help the disciples gain a deeper understanding of God, of each other, and of themselves.

Jesus and Peter

Jesus' *philia* relationship with Peter transformed Peter from an immature follower of Christ into the rock upon which Jesus built his church. Their spiritual friendship shaped both of their lives in a dramatic way. The two men shared their hearts, their intellect, their emotions, and their physical bonding, allowing them to receive validation, love, and affection from each other.[190]

When Jesus first encountered the man whom he would three years later call "the rock," he immediately changed Simon's name to Peter, something akin to what some priests or nuns do when taking their final vows promising complete obedience to God.[191]

Knowing one's name in the Jewish tradition was significant in that it reflected a familiarity and faithfulness that bonded two people together permanently. Hence, as with Jonathan and David, the hearts and minds of Jesus and Peter were immediately knit together by God in such a strong bond that they became totally committed to each other, a sign of true spiritual friendship.[192]

Halfway through their three-year friendship, Jesus, in a moment of despair, asked Peter to mirror back to him who Peter believed Jesus was. Christ's need to be validated by another man came just after he had been viciously attacked by the Pharisees, who claimed he was a false god. In this moment of vulnerability, Jesus asked Peter to speak the truth into Jesus so that Jesus might have the inner strength to contend with the brutal attacks of the religious hierarchy.

Proclaiming that Jesus was indeed the "Son of the living God,"[193] Peter reflected back to Jesus who he was. "This is who you are and how we experience you" was the core of what Jesus' friend proclaimed to him as truth. Peter's response was clearly inspired by the Spirit of God.[194] This exchange between the two men marked a significant shift in Peter's understanding of who his friend was and who Jesus was called by God to become. Their interconnection at this moment symbolized the very human need of Jesus to have his friend echo back to him who he was in a moment of crisis. "You are the son of God," Peter proclaimed, affirming not only the truth of who Jesus was, and is, but also the three-dimensional nature of their spiritual friendship: Jesus, Peter, and God.

In return, Jesus proceeded to tell Peter the truth of who Peter was. Jesus boldly proclaimed back to Peter, "And now I am going to tell you who you are, who you *really* are. You are Peter, a rock. This is the rock on which I will put together my church, a church so expansive with energy that not even the gates of hell will be able to keep it out."[195] Jesus' words confirmed the strength he saw in Peter, affirming Peter's gift of leadership.

This bond between men who mirror for each other who they are is precisely the path of spiritual friendship Jesus blazed for all men, a path to which men are being restored in the midst of the current crisis in masculinity.

In addition to words, Jesus often used the gift of touch to convey the depth of his love and acceptance to Peter. At the Transfiguration, the booming voice of God broke through the clouds, proclaiming Jesus as the Son of God in whom God takes great delight. Overtaken by the intensity of this encounter with

God and his prophets, Peter and the other disciples fell to the ground, shaking with fear. Sensing his friend's trepidation, Jesus reached down to comfort and reassure Peter, placing his strong and caring hands gently on Peter's face, coaxing him, "Don't be afraid."[196] The warmth of Jesus' touch on Peter's face brought Peter back to the reality of the moment, assuring him he was loved. He was safe.

At the Last Supper, Jesus chose to show his love for his friend by washing Peter's feet along with the feet of the other disciples. This unprecedented exchange between two men captured the depth of their love, ritualizing their friendship. In the Jewish tradition, it was common for a man to wash his feet before entering one's home so as not to dirty the home with dust from his sandals. A Jewish person might also wash their feet prior to saying their ritual prayers. However, a man would never wash another man's feet, according to Jewish tradition, unless he was a hired servant.[197]

The fact that Jesus chose to break Jewish tradition and wash Peter's feet symbolized the immensity of his love for Peter, his fidelity for him as a man, his joy in their deep and lasting friendship. Instead of a towel, Jesus used his apron to dry Peter's feet.[198] Through this ritual, Jesus displayed his willingness to give everything, including his whole heart and life, for his friend Peter.

Peter's initial reaction was typical of most men. He rejected Jesus' attempts to draw that close to him, demanding he would never let his friend break tradition and wash his feet. In contrast to the rich young man who walked away from Jesus' invitation to a deeper relationship, once Jesus explained his desire not to dominate Peter but rather to simply love and serve him at the deepest level of *philia* love, Peter surrendered his heart to his friend responding, "Then wash not only my feet, but also my hands. Wash my head!"[199]

After completing this ritual of *philia* love, Jesus invoked a spiritual blessing of protection over their friendship, praying that God's Spirit would pour out upon him and Peter. In that moment, Jesus named the Spirit of God that would soon come upon Peter and the other disciples as "another Friend" who was to be sent by the Father to be with them always:

I will talk to the Father, and he'll provide you another Friend so that you will always have someone with you. This Friend is the Spirit of Truth. The godless world can't take him in because it doesn't have eyes to see him, doesn't know what to look for. But you know him already because he has been staying with you, and will even be *in* you!...The Friend, the Holy Spirit whom the Father will send at my request, will make everything plain to you. He will remind you of all the things I have told you. I'm leaving you well and whole. That's my parting gift to you.[200]

Bestowing the gift of spiritual friendship upon Peter and the other apostles, one of the last earthly acts by Jesus before he died, established the foundation and the sacramental nature of spiritual friendships. Jesus rooted such friendships in their triune relationship: two human beings bonded together by God's Holy Spirit—the "Other Friend." One of the gifts that Jesus blessed Peter and all men with at this closing banquet was the gift of spiritual friendship, a friendship which "springs directly from God, who in the overflowing of his love created men to share his love by loving each other and himself."[201]

This triune nature of spiritual friendships was not only spoken with words by Jesus but modeled by him throughout his life as he embraced his deep friendship with Peter. The Other Friend, Jesus proclaimed with his life, is the source and foundation upon which all spiritual friendships are formed and from which they abide in God.

Jesus and Lazarus

The Gospel describes Jesus weeping openly after learning of the death of his dear friend Lazarus.[202] As the crowd watched Jesus mourning, many remarked, "Look how deeply he loved him."[203]

One can only imagine this carpenter's son standing alone outside the dusty grave of his beloved companion sobbing in unrestrained sorrow. The echo of his cries must have reverberated throughout the crowd, as they watched him in silence. The immensity of his love and magnitude of his loss poured from his heart with each tear as he expressed the depth of his pain.

This shortest passage found in Scripture, "Jesus wept," captures the essence of Christ's heart and the depth of the friendship between these two men. The Savior of the world, God's divine Son, a man of strength, power, and conviction, is brought to tears by the loss of a man he loved deeply.

One can only speculate what kind of love Jesus had for his dear friend Lazarus, since Scripture does not reveal much of their story. Despite the brevity of words about them, it is clear that Jesus' love for Lazarus was remarkable, given the profound impact his death had on Jesus.

The fact that Jesus chose to use his power to raise Lazarus from the dead suggests that perhaps Jesus needed Lazarus in a very human way. When Jesus came and visited Martha and Mary throughout the years, it would be reasonable to conclude that their brother Lazarus was there with them, sharing meals with Jesus, drinking wine, and telling stories about their adventures. Then retiring to the sitting room, their man cave, they shared their minds and hearts as only men can do in the company of other men.

Perhaps Jesus found in Lazarus during those quiet times the freedom and safety within their friendship to share his fears about the task his Father had given him to do. He may have confided in Lazarus how scared he was when the townsfolk tried to throw him off the cliff, demanding he leave the village for fear he would stir up more trouble. He might have shared the joy he felt when the crowd sat mesmerized, listening at his feet to the words of his sermon on the mountain, and he could tell they were finally getting it. Maybe he even shared how healing the touch of Mary Magdalene's tears felt on his feet when she caressed him and loved him as no other woman had.

One might wonder if after those times of deep sharing with his friend Lazarus, Jesus asked himself in the quiet of the late evening hours before he fell asleep, "Is it okay for me to love Lazarus this way? Is it okay for me to need another man's love and acceptance the way I need Lazarus's love and acceptance?" It might have been a haunting question for the Savior of the world. It may have even been a question he tried to hide from his Father, since men are not accustomed to needing anything or anyone, much less the *philia* love of another man.

Yet somewhere along the journey, long before Lazarus's death, Jesus perhaps resolved this daunting question. And the answer to his question, a question men seeking wholeness must entertain, may well have been: "Yes. Yes, it is okay for one man to cherish and need the love and acceptance of another man in a way that surpasses all understanding. It is okay to be interdependent upon other men when our hearts are knit together by God intellectually, emotionally, physically, and spiritually. It is the way God designed us as men—to need each other, to share our stories of love and life on the God-path."

Deep in every man's heart, we know all of this is true—true because Christ modeled this kind of love through his friendship with Lazarus.

His spiritual friendship with Lazarus displays Christ's willingness to share his life with a few select men on a deeper level, to experience the rawness of his emotions and share his vulnerability with these men, to live into the reality that strength and courage rise out of weakness and interdependence.[204] By sharing his emotional weakness, desperately needing Lazarus as his friend, Christ perhaps was able to access the power of God, allowing the Son of Man to raise his friend from the dead. In his weakness, the human Jesus found God's divine strength.

Pillar Two

It was not an exclusive friendship, but rather a preferential friendship that Jesus shared with his friends. Because it was not mutually exclusive, the friendship enhanced and supported the other primary relationships in each man's life.

Jesus enjoyed a preferential love for a limited number of men whom he trusted as his spiritual friends.[205] Lazarus, Peter, and John stand out as the three men for whom Jesus had a special affection.

Jesus confided more deeply in these men, spent more time with them, and leaned more heavily into his relationship with them for strength than he did the other disciples. He allowed them deeper access into his heart. They in turn allowed him deeper access into theirs.

John was called the "disciple whom Jesus loved," the one to whom Jesus entrusted his mother at his death. Peter was the one ready to wage battle to prevent his friend's death and to whom Jesus entrusted the church. Lazarus was the one whose death caused Jesus to weep, then, reeling from the loss of his love and deep affection, Jesus raised his friend from the dead through the power of his masculine strength and compassion.

Some theologians contend that this type of preferential love is contrary to the Christian message that love be offered equally to all. They claim there was no special form of love between Jesus and these men.[206]

However, *philia* love, by its very nature, is preferential. Scripture abounds with examples of how God himself had special friendships in the form of his unique relationships with Noah, Abraham, Moses, and David. David was called the "man after God's own heart."[207] Abraham is the only one in the Bible whom God refers to specifically as his friend.[208] The evidence of both God and his Son's life makes it clear that in addition to disciples, followers, and mere acquaintances, they considered two or three men spiritual friends.[209]

The implications are significant. If the Son of Man, who was both human and divine, needed a handful of special friends in his life with whom to walk his earthly journey, how much more must we need the same if we wish to follow his model? Jesus' unique friendships with John, Peter, and Lazarus enriched Christ's human life, mixing joy, laughter, and encouragement into his daily trek. This richness poured over into his other relationships, enhancing his ability to be fully present and engaged with his mother, Martha, Mary, and the twelve disciples. Christ's unique friendships supported the bond of affinity he had with the other people in his life.

Additionally, it is clear from the model of Christ's spiritual friendships that one of the goals of these special friendships is to promote each other's interdependence. In this sense, the friendships take on a sacramental quality: the human bearing the image of the divine. As a result, the friendships formed by God and sustained by God become a means of grace with extraordinary possibilities for growth in the life of Christ and deeper communion with God.[210] Theologically, spiritual friendships, "find their rootedness in communion with God which is found in and through communion with others who are in communion with God."[211] Our yearning for God strives toward its completion in and through one's spiritual friends. We experience "God with skin." God's love becomes flesh. God's love incarnates through the hearts and minds and souls of spiritual friends in relationship with each other.[212]

Spiritual friends form an inner circle of sacred trust with a limited number of men who are granted access to our hearts at the deepest level. These special relationships create the bedrock for growth and transformation into the image and likeness of God. Other more casual friends may very well be part of God's creative expression of love in and through one's life, but out of careful discernment, such acquaintances are not allowed to tap into the more vulnerable parts of our hearts.

The sacramental nature of spiritual friendships finds its expression in the ancient ritual of *adelphopoeseis*, the Greek term for the "making of brothers."[213] This ceremony was mainly practiced in Eastern Christianity, especially in the Greek Orthodox Church. This liturgical rite served as the formal means by which the church recognized and sanctified *philia* as a method of expressing God's kingdom in the world.[214] This deeply prayerful ceremony was intended to transform the human friendship into a spiritual friendship of brotherhood.[215] Many modern theologians suggest that this liturgical celebration should be restored[216] in the Christian church along with the Theology of Friendship, both of which were lost during the religious and cultural conflict rising from the Reformation and its Counter-Reformation.[217]

From a psychological perspective, the fact that Jesus had several spiritual friendships, instead of only one, suggests that exclusive friendships should be avoided to prevent codependency. An exclusive friendship carries the potential of turning the individuals into idols of each other, with the inherent risk of a person defining himself by the strength of their relationship. Healthy spiritual companions, in contrast, serve as icons pointing each other toward God, revealing the love of God for and through them. O'Callaghan writes:

> True friends relish the distance between them as much as the communion that unites them. A sound friendship will repudiate every movement to collapse that distance by coercing the identity of one's friend into the function of one's own.[218]

The perfect model of friendship exhibited by Christ envisions men who leave room for other spiritual friends; men who support and encourage the other relationships with which his friend has also committed his life and loyalty so that neither friend need be all things for the other.

Pillar Three

The friendship was formed naturally, there being an intuitive quality about it that suggests the friendship was initiated by and gifted to them from God.

In his book *Feast of Friendship*, Paul O'Callaghan describes the unexpected way in which spiritual friendships are often initially formed:

> The truth of Jesus' intimacy with John demonstrates the fact that certain persons are naturally drawn to other persons by a fundamental kinship of spirit. The result is the formation of a preferential relationship between them. They will experience closeness that few, if any, others will be able to share. Such friends may not readily understand what is occurring between them at first. It is an intuitive connection between hearts that may be unexpected or outwardly unlikely. Yet its depth and power are undeniable from the outset.[219]

This element of surprise is a critical part in discerning whether the friendship is bestowed by God as a spiritual friendship. God's Spirit is always initiating movement toward good in our lives, writes Father Richard Hauser, S.J. Our job is to recognize the movement of God and respond in tune with God's grace.[220]

A helpful tool in determining if something or someone is brought into our lives through the movement of God's grace instead of through mere chance is the existence of the element of surprise. When God's grace is the source of the movement, there is often a sense of serendipity, a sense that a sacred person suddenly appeared in one's life as if he or she was part of an unfolding pattern. The serendipity seems to have chosen us. When such a meeting between two strangers occurs, it is often unlikely, unplanned, or unexpected, leading one to conclude it has traces of God's fingerprints all over it.[221]

In addition to the element of surprise, a natural and immediate bond often arises between spiritual friends. This natural drawing of hearts is described in the relationship between Jonathan and David. "Their hearts were knit together as brothers from the very moment they met,"[222] Scripture reports. It was as if the two men had known each other since birth.

The same kindred spirit immediately arose in the relationship between Jesus and Peter. Jesus changed Simon's name to Peter within the first few moments of their initial greeting—a sign of their deep connection from the outset.[223]

Many individuals who have formed spiritual friendships report a similar sense that they had known each other for years. They are surprised by the high level of commonality and connection they experienced immediately in terms of the four posts of spiritual friendships: intellectual, emotional, physical, and spiritual. Some men even joke that perhaps they were twin brothers, but got switched into different families at birth.

In His Fullness, a men's ministry,[224] often encourages two men who are part of a spiritual friendship to rate the level of connection they experience with each other on a scale of 1–10 with respect to the four posts. This inventory allows the two friends to better understand and discuss the nature of their friendship and its unique characteristics.

The core question for men forming a *philia* friendship asks, "Is this friendship a gift from God?" This question is fundamental since, as Aelred of Rievaulx reminds us, spiritual friendships are formed out of pure love and have as their foundation the love of God. But Aelred cautions that a spiritual friend ought to be chosen with utmost care and discerned with extreme caution.[225]

As the friendship evolves, Aelred believes four qualities in a friend must be tested with ongoing discernment: loyalty, right intention, discretion, and patience.[226] Loyalty demands that each friend hold the highest good of the other in utmost esteem. Right intention means that one can expect nothing from the friendship except God and the other friend's natural good. Discretion requires that one strive to understand one's friend, including his strengths and weaknesses, and have the courage to celebrate his strengths and help correct his shortcomings. Finally, patience demands that each friend must be willing to bear every adversity for his friend.[227]

If the above four qualities continue to exist within the friendship, Aelred would suggest the friends are well on their way toward forming a long-lasting spiritual friendship. However, one final pillar is necessary to keep the spiritual friendship on track.

Pillar Four

The friends' primary focus is on helping each other walk closely with God in the day-to-day events of their lives.

I'm in love with my God.
And my God's in love with me.
And the more I love you the more I know
that I'm in love with my God.[228]

These song lyrics rolled off the tongue of Father Donald Joyce, a round, red-haired, ruddy-cheeked Irish Catholic priest skipping rope at recess with a group of sixth grade boys and girls at an elementary school I attended as a youth. As Father Joyce sang these words, a smile as big as Christmas morning radiated from his face with every skip of the rope.

The song captures the essence of spiritual friendships: two friends in love with God; God in love with them; and the more they experience the love of each other, the more they experience the love of God.

The essence of Jesus' life is captured by this song. For Jesus, everything was spiritual. Everything he did focused on listening to and following in God's footsteps. His focus, the lens through which he viewed his life, was through his relationship with God.

In order to be fully divine, he must have also lived to become fully human. His life evolved. He was transformed and formed by each of his life experiences and the relationships he entered into like any other human.

His spiritual friendships with John, Peter, and Lazarus shaped Jesus' identity as a human being and he shaped theirs. They rubbed off on each other just as Father Joyce's joy rubbed off on me as he sang his love song to God. Jesus, John, Peter, and Lazarus were all spiritual mentors for each other. They helped each other listen to their own lives. They encouraged each other "to recognize God's amazing threads of grace at work in their life that formed a tapestry like none other."[229]

These spiritual friends invested themselves in each other. They gave a part of their lives and created space and time to nurture each man's spirit. Together as friends, they encouraged each other to reach and long for more. They helped each other recognize they had a story to share, a song to sing which was uniquely their own, given to them by God. Through the *philia* love of their friendship, God integrated his Spirit in and through these men so that they might become one heart and mind in him.[230]

Jesus was able to experience the love of God through the lives of his friends. John, Peter, and Lazarus provided Jesus with both the safety and the power for Jesus to discover, grow into, and use his human gifts as teacher and fisher of men. His God-centered spiritual friendships formed and empowered Jesus, allowing him to find his unique voice and human gifts, then use them to serve as a spiritual mentor for others.

Strengthened by the steel of his spiritual friendships, Jesus mentored others such as Martha and Mary and the twelve apostles, empowering them to discover through holy listening and holy seeing their unique part in God's salvation story.[231] God's plan for establishing His kingdom here on earth became a deeper reality through the simple means of creating relationships—rich, creative human bonds, pointing toward God, sustained by and through God.

This manner of building God's kingdom here on earth, one relationship at a time, is described in the book *Spiritual Mentoring*:

> The kind of teaching Jesus provided them was very different from the classroom instruction of the academy today. It assumed a relationship and style that made different demands on both rabbi and disciple, teacher and learner, mentor and protégé. More like the work of the craftsmen tutoring the young apprentice, Jesus' style of instruction embodied a pedagogy that invested life in the learner through an incarnation of the message being taught. This teaching was not something that was conceptually defined for his disciples as much as it was lived, experienced, tasted and touched by the learners. Jesus not only spent time instructing, training and informing; he spent much time *forming a community*.
>
> In the sweat of shared work as well as the dusty exertion of shared travel, they were always in the classroom. By the sea with wriggling, smelly and oily fish in their hands, in the fields with the crunch of fresh wheat snapped from stalks swaying in the hot Palestinian sun, even in the stimulation of the sensual barrage of the city with its crowds, bazaars, buildings, soldiers, markets—they were always in school, always becoming a community of learners whom he called disciples. "Follow me," he said to them. A world of meaning reverberates in the simple words of his call. Even the language of "call" is intensely related to Jesus' strategy of choosing, nurturing, and developing an inner circle of disciples to whom he would give unique authority to teach the next generation of followers.[232]

After spending his human life creating and modeling both spiritual friendships and mentoring relationships here on earth, Jesus, at the end of his life, then gave each man and woman the mission of forming their own spiritual bonds with others through the words of the Great Commission: "Go out and train everyone you meet, far and near, in this way of life, marking them by baptism in the threefold name: Father, Son, and Holy Spirit."[233]

The call of Christ's Great Commission is twofold: first, surround oneself with spiritual friends who will help you discover your unique gifts and empower you to use them for God's ongoing creation here on earth; second, become spiritual mentors in relationship with others who are willing to hear God's call to follow him.

There is no strategy, no marketing plan or committee, no great series of sermons which can create this type of deep and lasting relationship. The kingdom of God here on earth can only be found by following in the footsteps of Christ, imitating what he did and how he lived.

Jesus' friendships with John, Peter, and Lazarus pointed him and them toward God. They were focused on God, moved toward God. Their focus on God formed the core of their lives. God is what they talked about when they got up in the morning. God is who they noticed was transforming them and others as they moved through their day. God is the one they thanked as they went to bed at night. Daily, God incarnated God's self in and through each of them. The more Jesus, John, Peter, and Lazarus fell in love with each other as friends through the ups and downs of their shared lives, the more each of them fell more deeply in love with God.

It is that simple. Relationship. And the focus on God of Jesus' relationships provides us with an inner compass—a centering point for our own spiritual friendships. If, like Jesus, the friendships we have been gifted with are spiritual friendships, they will point us and our friends toward God. We will find more of God and of our truest self in the midst of these transforming friendships. We will become the incarnation of God's love for and through each other. And if the primary focus of those friendships shifts away from God as their center—toward lust or envy or simply toward the pursuit of pleasure or greater adventure—then we can discern that those friendships are no longer spiritual friendships or never were spiritual from the start.

"The glory of God is man fully alive," writes St. Irenaeus.[234] This invitation to the fullness of life through the experience of rich spiritual friendships is patterned after the life of Christ. Jesus taught his friends how to pray; he then prayed for and with his friends. He taught them how to gain deeper trust in God. Jesus found time, despite the demands on him, to find solitude to be alone with his Father. He never distracted himself with his friendships. His final prayer for his friends at the Last Supper marked the primary goal of his relationship with his friends: that they would be one with God as he was one with God.[235] In that final prayer, he spoke what the next few days of his life would reveal: there is no greater love than to lay down (or as in the original Greek: to set forth) one's life for one's friends.[236]

As men and pastoral counselors and those involved in men's ministry, we can help point ourselves and other men toward the freedom of this path of spiritual friendship, a path that Jesus embodied. We might nudge those with whom we befriend and counsel to seek out and find the God-centered friendships men need in order to be transformed. We might evaluate our current friendships to see if they are God-centered.

We can also create safe space by establishing small sacred circles of men who join together on a regular basis to pray and share their journey together from which spiritual friendships might unfold and be formed. We might help restore the theology of friendship which has been lost in the crush of post-modernism. Perhaps our generation of men, pastoral counselors, and men's spirituality ministers are invited by God to help restore spiritual friendships as a path toward wholeness, a path which the rich young man was looking for, but for which he neither had the courage nor the wisdom to pursue.

CHAPTER 8
IMPLICATIONS FOR MINISTRY

Men are in the midst of a major cultural and spiritual shift. Patriarchy has been laid to rest. The old definitions of what it means to be a man have been abandoned. As a result, transformation is upon us. The men's movement is slowly growing. The deep male is emerging.

To accomplish the inner work necessary for the courageous journey into this form of new manhood, men need fresh language, creative tools, and powerful encouragement to keep focused on the necessary tasks of transformation. Men and those who counsel with them and those who wish to embrace the men's movement and its energy are invited to view men's issues through a new lens: the lens of masculine spirituality—a spirituality which is different and unique from women's spirituality and which has been badly misshaped and distorted by culture. Masculine spirituality calls men to the ongoing endeavor of developing and deepening their relationship with God in the company of other men.

According to Thomas Merton, the purpose of the spiritual life is "to penetrate beneath the surface of a man's life, to get behind the facade of conventional gestures and attitudes which he presents to the world, and to bring out his inner spiritual freedom, his inmost truth, which is what we call the likeness of Christ in his soul."[237]

Men, men's ministry leaders, and pastoral counselors have a unique opportunity to create the sacred places to find and nurture their souls in the company of other men, as Merton suggests. This spiritual caretaking can be accomplished in a variety of settings: within our own spiritual friendships we share with other men; one-on-one in pastoral counseling and spiritual direction; through men's groups focusing on male spirituality issues and topics; and through encouraging other men to form spiritual friendships, helping create circles of men who will continue to walk shoulder to shoulder with one another as they engage life on its day-to-day terms.

While each of these settings provides rich seed for growth, the real work of transformation embeds itself and continues in daily relationship with others who are also on the spiritual path. That is why it is crucial for spiritual friendships to be understood, encouraged, and fostered. In short, relationships matter.

If these God-given friendships are to gain greater acceptance and understanding as a critical tool for men's transformation, we as men, as men's ministry leaders, and as counselors will need to study the history, theology, and theory underlying them. Equipped with new-found wisdom concerning these types of relationships, we can then in turn teach others about these unique friendships, inviting men to develop spiritual friendships in the same way Jesus walked in relationship with Peter, John, and Lazarus. We can also gain a deeper understanding of the man rules, recognizing how damaging these cultural norms are to us and other men and encouraging men to break the shackles forged on them by these remnants of patriarchy.

The Spirit of God in the midst of these changing times is inviting men to learn and teach others about the theology of spiritual friendships: where they came from; what they looked like in the lives of Christ and our spiritual fathers; how we lost them; and how we might regain the gift of male friendships for ourselves, and for our sons who are looking for us to hand them a better world than our fathers handed us.

So, "How do we do that?" we might ask. "How do we create sacred space for men to develop and deepen their relationship with God in the company of other men?" The answer: "We don't. The Holy Spirit does." We simply discern and cooperate with God's grace.

Cooperation with God's grace, however, can have framework—concrete vision that we can lean into as we allow grace to move in and through us. One vision is to form men's ministries that will create safe, small communities of men where there is room for God—and room for men to pursue and explore their souls.

An example we might look to is a ministry called Over the Edge, which started in Michigan in 2010 as the result of many years of inner work by its cofounders. Over the Edge (OTE) was created after its founders realized there were few, if any, places where men could gather together to discuss their spirituality, their sexuality, and the unique issues men face in modern culture. In fact, the spiritual life center that the founders were part of had initially declared that men did *not* need nor would the institution permit men to form a separate ministry. The center's resistance rose out of an underlying fear that such exclusivity might encourage the same patriarchy that had hampered women's growth and development over the years.

Undaunted by the spiritual life center's refusal to create space for men to do their inner work in the company of other men, the OTE founders decided to go ahead and form their own men's ministry as a separate nonprofit group. With no traditional ministry or business plan in place, the men simply decided to let the Holy Spirit guide them, praying Thomas Merton's prayer of discernment: "Lord I have no idea where I am going. I don't even know if I am on the right path. But, I trust my desire to follow you will indeed be enough to guide me."

With the Holy Spirit as their guide and Kevin Costner's *Field of Dreams* movie mantra, "If you build it they will come," in their hearts, OTE initially offered an eight-week workshop for men using the *Fathered by God* DVD series developed by John Eldredge. With embellishment to fit the participants' needs and background, OTE made its initial plunge by offering the series at a local Methodist church. Fifteen men signed up for the initial series. They quickly embraced the inner work required to journey through the six male archetypes outlined by Eldredge and his band of spiritual friends on the DVD: beloved son, cowboy, warrior, lover, king, and sage.

The depth of sharing by the fifteen men was astounding. Each week they discussed their joys, strengths, journey and struggles as men. Each man commented they had never experienced such an opportunity to open up with other men in a safe and sacred space. At the end of the eight weeks, the men begged for more—more masculine spirituality, more opportunities to dig deep and explore their inner masculine gifts and energy with other men.

In response to the group's desires, OTE began a monthly group spiritual direction meeting. Using the model of *lectio divina* developed by the Dominican Spiritual Life Center,[238] eight men, some from the Fathered by God workshop and others new to OTE, committed to meet once a month for six months to share their journey in a prayerful contemplative model.

Once again the comments from each participant were remarkable. The depth of sharing was immense—so much so that the men teased each other that they had the "balls to break the man code." At the end of the six months, the group decided to continue meeting for another six months and to invite two new men who had expressed an interest in the group to join them. The group has been meeting now for over a year and a half.

With the sowing of these initial seeds and a new leadership team in place at the spiritual life center, OTE next decided to bring the concept of forming a men's ministry back to the spiritual life center for reconsideration. To their surprise, the proposal now met with acceptance.

In the fall of 2010, OTE offered the Fathered by God series at the spiritual life center. After an article appeared in a local newspaper discussing the unique new men's movement and the upcoming series, twelve men signed up, journeying together in the same band-of-brothers style for eight weeks. The final class included a rite of passage where one by one, each man was initiated into their masculine strength as God's beloved, filled with their male gifts of the beloved son, cowboy, warrior, lover, king, and sage.

In the winter of 2011, OTE created and offered another workshop titled *Listening for God Knows What—How God Speaks to Men in Unique Ways*. This workshop was designed to teach men discernment in a practical and experiential way. Pulling together a number of resources from several authors on such topics as learning to hear God's voice through nature, spiritual friendships, dreams, prayer, and Scripture, the group formed a safe and sacred community as the men studied, prayed, and learned to discern together for eight weeks.

One of the key components that formed each workshop meeting was an initial "check-in," where each man was invited to share how his week had been in terms of his prayer life and his relationship with God. This check-in time was well received. It offered an opportunity for each of the men to stop, look back, and reflect on their week through a spiritual lens. It also gave the men an opportunity to learn more from and about each other. The men encouraged each other verbally during this time as they shared their journeys and together broke the man rules.

Characteristic of the other workshops, the men in this group also asked to continue meeting after the initial eight weeks. The men decided to create their own format and agreed to rotate the weekly role of facilitator. They created a loose structure for each meeting consisting of a check-in, prayer, and discussion on a topic related to men's spirituality presented by that week's facilitator.

Excited by the men's enthusiasm around these initial offerings, OTE decided it was time to pull together a larger group of men to discuss and shape what the future of men's spirituality at the spiritual life center might look like. With the assistance of several women on staff at the center, the center set up a gathering of men called "A Morning of Reflection and Conversation about Men's Spirituality." The center and OTE compiled an email database of men who had expressed an interest in men's spirituality. They then sent out an email blast with an open invitation to attend the gathering. The response was overwhelming. More than sixty men showed up for the Saturday morning event.

The format for the morning of reflection and conversation was simple and experiential. (A detailed agenda of the day is attached as Appendix 2.) After introductions, prayer, and background, the men were invited to spend twenty minutes in quiet reflection, pondering their lives in decades. To help focus the time, the men were given a sheet with this exercise:

The Making of a Man
Divide your life into 10-year segments:
Ages: 0-10; 10-20; 20-30; 30-40; 40-50; 50-60; 60-70; 70-80+.

For each decade of your life, reflect on the following:

1. Recall one or two challenges and accomplishments that helped "make a man out of you."

2. Name one or two people who were significant to you at this time in your life.

3. What or who do you wish you had in your life at that time that might have made it easier?

After the participants completed this piece, they formed small groups based upon the decade they wished to explore more deeply that morning. In their small groups, the men discussed the results of their personal reflection time. They were also given a fourth question to address and report back to the larger group: "What might the center offer to help you and other men celebrate their accomplishments and meet their challenges throughout the various stages of life?"

The small group sharing was one of the highlights of the day. The men openly discussed with each other their wounds, their fears, their joys, and their desires as they addressed each question. After thirty minutes of lively conversation, the small groups were then called back to the large group session, where the men reported back on what they had discussed in connection with the fourth question they had been given.

The large group session provided a plethora of information and insight from the men for OTE and for the center to use as it moved forward in establishing a men's spirituality ministry. The information was tabulated into a final report made available to the men at a later date. The men made it clear through their comments that what they had experienced that morning was powerful and transforming. More importantly, they said they did not want the energy of the day to end.

One of the many fruits of the morning of reflection was the desire of the group to create a men's spirituality leadership team to form and keep the ministry moving forward. The participants envisioned a small group of interested men who would join together to pray, discern, and implement many of the ideas generated that day. Eighteen men volunteered to serve on that leadership team.

In response, a morning of leadership discernment was organized within several weeks and carried out by one of the center's staff. At that follow-up leadership meeting, the men were invited to discern what the role of the leadership team would be, what gifts each member should have to be part of the team, and who of the eighteen would be best suited to serve on the team.

From the eighteen men, eight discerned a call to serve on the leadership team. The team then created a vision statement around their working definition of men's spirituality: "The ongoing endeavor to develop and deepen our relationship with God in the company of other men."

The team decided it would meet quarterly to pray together, discern, and develop programs and experiences for men to move deeper into their faith. It was anticipated this leadership team would provide a foundation and springboard for the growth and development of the men's spirituality ministry at the center in collaboration with OTE. Although the men's spirituality ministry was just getting started, it was hoped that it would provide a strong foundation for creating the sacred space and opportunities needed for men to grow in the company of other men.

In addition to the above, OTE had begun dialoguing with other faith communities in the Grand Rapids, Michigan, area about the possibility of jointly sponsoring an ecumenical men's spirituality conference each year. The annual gathering would bring men together to grow deeper in their spirituality. Instead of simply creating a one-day event without any follow-up, each faith community that would help to sponsor the annual event would be invited to offer a follow-up series in their faith community shortly after the conference.

The overall goal of OTE is to provide a safe place and opportunity for men to do their inner work of transformation. It is the desire of OTE that by offering numerous opportunities for men to join together and explore their faith, their spirituality, and their unique gifts as men, the Holy Spirit will continue to initiate the inner growth each man needs, resulting in their own transformation and the transformation of the communities in which they live. It is also envisioned that spiritual friendships will form among the men who attend these various men's gatherings as they experience their common bond as men on the God-path.

What OTE is discovering is that men, if given the opportunity, *want* to form community with other men who are serious about exploring the God-path and are *willing* to do the inner work to realize their full potential. The job of pastoral counselors and men's spirituality groups is to create those opportunities—to create the sacred space so that men can go deeper in the company of other men. Most importantly, by letting the men form the ministry, instead of trying to impose a cookie-cutter program on them, adequate room is left for the Holy Spirit to create the unique space and experience.

A sampling of men's responses from the various workshops outlined above best express men's desire and willingness to dig deep spiritually when afforded the chance:

> "This workshop created an environment that made it safe for each of us to go deep. To trust each other. To care for each other and to move into those dark places within ourselves in a prayerful way surrounded by the care and concern of other men."
>
> "I learned for the first time how important daily prayer is and how to do it. By journeying together these past eight weeks and sharing each week how our prayer life was going, I felt invited and challenged to become serious about prayer because I experienced the peace it brought to my busy life. I don't want to stop now when I have just begun to move so much deeper into my own self and my relationship with God. I need the other guys in this group to continue to walk with me on this journey and will do anything it takes to make our group an ongoing reality."

OTE has come to realize that God's Spirit works in amazing ways if we will co-create with God and open the door with opportunities for men to sharpen their iron together. Men congregate in bars, on basketball courts, and around big-screen TV sets, watching major sports events, because they want and need to connect with each other. It is the way God designed us—for deep male connection and relationship with other men.

Society and even the church, however, have not offered men the avenues to connect beyond these culturally safe and superficial ways. Like the rich young man, men are still looking for wholeness. Men are looking for meaningful relationship; that is how God hard-wired men. It is up to us as men, pastoral counselors, and men's spirituality leaders to create those opportunities for God's Spirit to meet men where they are so that they can continue to grow and be transformed.

"If you build it, they will come." And they did, OTE discovered. But, we have to seek and invite in order to find what we are looking for. We have to create meaningful sacred space for the rich young man to walk away from the allure of his riches to sit down and spend time creating relationship with his "true self" and with God.

OTE is only one of many ways to create sacred space for men to do the necessary work of transformation. God's Spirit is initiating in all of us, whether we are pastoral counselors, men in the marketplace, or common folk in the pews. God invites us to say "Yes" in response to God's ongoing invitation to "come, follow me."

We can either walk away like the rich young man did and continue to experience emptiness, isolationism, or, worse yet, continue to deny men's legitimate God-given gifts and needs, or we can listen with our whole heart, mind, and body to where God is inviting us, to that place of the deep male, where men are free to express their needs and desires to connect with God and each other.

Men deserve much more than the watered-down culture they are getting from society, from the church, and from pastoral counselors. God's Spirit is guiding us each step of the way as we move through this transformative time in history. However, to grow through and emerge from this time of grace, we must listen to the heartbeat of Christ beating softly within our own chest and within the chest of our spiritual friends and brothers.

CHAPTER 9
AN END AND A BEGINNING

James B. Nelson says that writers write not because they know something significant but because they have questions they want to wrestle with and answer, and so they do, on paper. Researching and writing this book has been part of my inner wrestling. It has taken me years to listen to the inner voice that is inviting me to follow him, more than half a lifetime to discover my unique gifts of writing and teaching, and more than a decade to begin using those gifts in a way that is life-giving for me and, hopefully, for others.

When I began this project, I was overwhelmed. There was too much information to process and too much time that needed to be pulled away from my sixty-hour work week as a lawyer. When the alarm rang at 4:30 a.m., beckoning me to get up, pray, and write before I left for work at 8:00 a.m., I often resisted, made excuses, turned over in bed, demanding I needed more sleep. Much like the rich young man, I was ready many times to walk away from this book, willing to cash in my dreams for the illusion of an ordinary life.

Yet something inside of me drew me to keep writing, keep digging, keep doing the inner work that has spilled out both onto these pages and into my life. Midway through the research for this book, when I was just about ready to call it quits for good, God surprised me with a spiritual friend. He is a writer, a man on the God-path, and someone with whom we connect as a ten on all four posts of the pillars of spiritual friendship. The gift of his friendship, together with my wife and my two other spiritual friends, was the grace I needed to keep going.

My spiritual friend spoke words of truth to me. He told me I am a writer. He encouraged me to keep moving forward with my manuscript one day at a time. He simply loved me with his masculine strength and spirit when I was ready to quit and throw in the towel.

My spiritual friends have also encouraged me in my relationship with my wife. They have helped me become a better husband and father, told me they were not going to help me pack when I was ready to call it quits on my marriage. These men have helped me find the courage and wisdom to name and surrender many of the ghosts of my false self. Perhaps most of all, I have experienced God incarnate and his love for me through my spiritual friends and the love of my wife. God has revealed his love for me through the skin of their presence in my life.

Never in my wildest dreams could I have fashioned friends for my soul like God has fashioned for me. I pray I am half as good of a spiritual friend for them as they are for me. I know that I am a better man because of my friends and that they are truly a gift from God.

My prayer is that those who read this book will also have the courage or perhaps, like me, the desperation to pray that God would place at least one man in his life who will be his spiritual friend. I pray that the trickle of men who are willing to push against the man rules and "ask so that we might receive" will burst into a life-giving river, filled with an abundance of men willing to walk the God-path, shoulder to shoulder.

We are designed for more as men than the false gods and bits of table scraps society has allowed us to worship and eat. It is time we take the male journey together. It is time to dig deep into our masculine strength, get angry, and demand we be given what our souls have been promised.

We *are* the rich young men. And I believe that individually, and as a community, our hearts are already leading us—and that someday, in God's perfect timing, with God's abundant grace, our feet will catch up with our masculine souls.

Appendix 1
Order for Making Brothers

A rough and fairly literal translation of the ritual used in the early Christian church to bless a spiritual friendship. A more elegant translation, alongside the original Latin is provided by Alan Bray in his book, *The Friend*.

Introit:

We have received, God, thy mercy in the midst of thy temple. According to thy name, God, so also is thy praise to the ends of the earth. Thy right hand is full of righteousness.

Psalm:

Great is the Lord and exceedingly worthy to be praised in the city of our God in his holy mountain.

Glory be to the Father and to the Son and to the Holy Spirit.

As it was in the beginning and now and always and in ages of ages. Amen.

Lord have mercy, Christ mercy, Lord have mercy.

Our father ... and do not lead us into temptation.

Response: But deliver us from evil.

Make thy servants safe, my God, those who hope in thee. Send them aid, Lord, from the holy one. And from Zion watch over them, watch over them.

Lord, hear my prayer. And let my cry come unto thee.

The Lord be with you. And with thy spirit.

Prayer:

Through the intercession for us and for you of the blessed and glorious Mary, mother of the eternally only-begotten son of God, and of blessed Peter the prince of the apostles, to whom the Lord gave power in heaven and earth to bind and to loose and to dismiss the sins of the people, may He absolve you of all your sins past present and future and deliver you from all evil. Through Jesus Christ our Lord. Amen.

Prayer:

God, who gave thine apostles the command that through holy divinity they should call one another brothers, and who established Peter and Paul, and James and John, as brothers, bless these thy servants N and N [insert names of spiritual friends], who establish each other as brothers in thy name, so that through thee they may in turn from now on and in the future be worthy to be crowned. Through Jesus Christ our Lord. Amen.

Prayer:

Our almighty God, who art before the ages and wilt remain for ages of ages, who deigned to visit the human race through the womb of the Mother of God and virgin Mary, send thy holy angel upon these thy servants N and N that they may love one another, just as thy holy apostles Peter and Paul loved one another, and Andrew and James, John and Thomas, James, Philip, Matthew, Simon, Thaddeus and Matthias, and the holy martyrs Sergius and Bacchus, and Cosmas and Damian, not by carnal love, but by faith and the love of the Holy Spirit, that they may remain in that love all the days of their life. Through Jesus Christ our Lord. Amen.

Appendix 1

Epistle:

Choose and read an appropriate scripture from the Old Testament on the gift of friendship.

Tract:

Behold how good and how pleasant it is to dwell as brothers in one. Just like the ointment on his head which descended to his beard, the beard of Aaron.

Gospel:

Choose and read an appropriate scripture from the Gospel.

Communion chant:

Behold how good and how pleasant it is to dwell as brothers in one.

Prayer:

Lord God, our ruler, who made man in thine image and likeness, who ordered thy holy apostles Philip and Bartholomew to become brothers, not joined by worldly custom, but by faith and the Holy Spirit, and in the same way deigned to call the holy martyrs Sergius and Bacchus brothers, bless these thy servants N and N, not joined by worldly custom, but by faith and the Holy Spirit, grant that there may be love without hatred and without scandal between them all the days of their life, through the intercession of the holy Mother of God and Virgin Mary and of blessed N and N and of all the saints, because it behooves us to give thee all honour and glory, and to worship the Father and the Son and the Holy Spirit now and always and through infinite ages of ages. Amen.

Appendix 2
A Morning of Conversation and Reflection on Men's Spirituality

Schedule

9 – 9:50
Welcome; Bill Cosby Video—fathers and sons; Ice Breaker: Who was your childhood hero?

9:50 – 10:00
Opening Prayer.

10 – 10:30
Personal Reflection Exercise:

The Making of a Man

Divide your life into 10 year segments:
Ages: 0-10; 10-20; 20-30; 30-40; 40-50; 50-60; 60-70; 70-80+.

For each decade of your life reflect on the following:

Recall one or two challenges and accomplishments that helped "make a man out of you."

Name one or two people who were significant to you at this time in your life.

What or who do you wish you had in your life at that time that might have made it easier?

10:30 – 11:00
Small Group Sharing:
Gather into small groups depending upon the decade you wish to focus on this morning.

Small Group Discussion Questions

For the life decade that you choose to focus on today, share and discuss with your group:

What were one or two challenges and accomplishments in that decade that helped "make a man out of you?"

Who were the one or two people that were significant to you during that decade?

What or who do you wish you had in your life during that decade that might have made it easier?

What might the Center offer to help you and other men celebrate their accomplishments and meet their challenges throughout the various stages of life?

11:00 – 11:30
Large Group Discussion Question

Large Group Sharing: What might the Center offer to help men celebrate their accomplishments and meet their challenges throughout the various stages of life?

11:30 – 11:50
Moving Forward

Discernment: where do we go from here? Hand out written evaluations and input sheets. Allow time for men to fill out. Ask men to indicate if they are interested in being considered for the men's spirituality leadership team and, if so, to provide contact information on the input sheets.

11:50 – 12 noon
Closing Prayer.

End Notes

Introduction

1. Martin Pable, *The Quest for the Male Soul* (Notre Dame: Ave Maria Press, Inc., 1996), 8.
2. Luke 18:18-27. Mt 19:16-22. All biblical references throughout this work are from *The Message: The Bible in Contemporary Language,* translated by Eugene H. Peterson (Colorado Springs: NavPress, 2005).
3. Jan Halper, *Quiet Desperation: The Truth about Successful Men* (New York: Warner Books, 1988).
4. While the term, "masculine spirituality" can and has been defined in many ways, a good working definition might be the following: Men's ongoing endeavor to develop and deepen their relationship with God. See Pable, 1996, 15.
5. Patrick Arnold, *Wildmen, Warriors and Kings* (New York: Crossroad, 1995), 1.
6. Richard Rohr, *On the Threshold of Transformation* (Chicago: Loyola Press, 2010), xv-xvi.
7. Rohr 2010, xvi.
8. Rohr 2010, x.
9. Arnold 1995, 52.
10. Suzanne Fields, "When Manly Virtue Died," The *Grand Rapids Press*, 22 November 2011, sec. A, page 11.
11. Arnold 1995, 1.
12. Arnold 1995, 2.
13. Arnold 1995, 67.
14. David Murrow, *Why Men Hate Going to Church* (Nashville: Thomas Nelson Press, 2005).
15. Mark Walstrom, "*Men's Spirituality: Discovering our Myths and Remembering Ourselves.*" http://www.markwalstrom.com/articles/mens-spirituality.html (2010).
16. Arnold 1995, 67.
17. Carol Lee Flinders, *Rebalancing the World* (New York: HarperCollins Publishers, 2000).
18. Aelred of Rievaulx (St) 1147, *Spiritual Friendship,* translated by Mary Eugenia Laker; introduction by Douglas Roby (Kalamazoo: Cistercian Press, 1977).
19. Brian Patrick McGuire, *Friendship and Community, the Monastic Experience, 350-1250* (Ithaca: Cornell University Press, 2010). Brian Patrick McGuire finds that in seeking friends and friendship, medieval men and women sought self-knowledge, the enjoyment of life, the commitment of community, and the experience of God.

20 "Only in the twentieth century has [the doctrine of spiritual friendship] received its share of popular attention. As modern moral theology has turned away from the abstract and defensive attitude of handbook scholasticism, and as modern religions have turned their attention to the social implications of the Christian life, there has been a revival of interest in [the doctrine of] the Spiritual Friendship." Aelred of Rievaulx (St) 1147, 40.

21 In *The Feast of Friendship,* Paul D. O'Callaghan suggests that the church needs to return to the roots of its "Theology of Friendship." Paul D. O'Callaghan, *The Feast of Friendship* (Wichita: Eight Day Press, 2002). The doctrine of spiritual friendship appears to have been lost in the late Middle Ages and in the Counter-Reformation where the church developed a "mistrust" of particular friendships. Aelred of Rievaulx (St) 1147, 40.

Chapter One
22 Hanna Rosin, "The End of Men," *The Atlantic* (July/August, 2010).
23 Rosin, 2010.
24 Ken Cedeno, "Is God Dead?" *Time* (April 8, 1966).
25 Matt Sayles, "Men's Lib," *Newsweek* (September 20, 2010).
26 See: http://www.macmillandictionary.com/buzzword/entries/retrosexual.html.
27 See: http://www.media-awareness.ca/english/issues/stereotyping/men_and_masculinity/masculinity_stereotypes.cfm.
28 Boyson Hodgson, "The New Macho," http://journeytomanhood.blogspot.com/2010/10/new-macho.html. (Man-Making Blog, October 20, 2010).
29 Robert Bly, *Iron John: A Book about Men* (Cambridge: Da Cappa Press, 1990).
30 Bly 1990, 1.
31 Bly 1990, 1.
32 Bly 1990, 2.
33 Bly 1990, 2-3.
34 Peter M. Nardi, *Men's Friendships, Research on Men and Masculinities.* Newbury Park: Sage Publications, 1992), 4.
35 C. S. Lewis, *The Four Loves* (New York: Harcourt , Brace, 1960).
36 James B. Nelson, *The Intimate Connection: Male Sexuality, Masculine Spirituality* (Philadelphia: Westminster Press, 1988), 63.
37 Nelson 1988, 56. According to Nelson, men have been culturally forced to begin living "the lie of my own self-sufficiency, the lie that I have strength to be giver only, the lie that I never need to receive. The deception buttresses my need to control, for when I am the giver and the other is the only needy one, I am secure in my superiority. Truly, the words men

End Notes

often find hardest to speak are: 'I want. I need. I can't. I am afraid.'" Yet the women's movement demanded men get in touch with their softer side.

38 Bly 1990, 2-3.
39 Bly 1990, 2-3.
40 Bly 1990, 2-3.
41 Murrow, 2010, 141, 155.
42 Bly 1990, 14, 28-29.
43 Murrow, 2010, 106.
44 Murrow 2010, 106.
45 Bly, 1990, 6.
46 Murrow 2010, 139.
47 Ephesians 3:14-19.
48 Matt 13:45, 46.
49 Bly 1990, 4-6. The author will use the term "deep male" throughout this book as the term to describe the next step men must take individually and collectively on their masculine journey toward wholeness.

Chapter Two

50 The names and certain facts in this case study have been changed to preserve confidentiality.
51 Ann Lamott in her book *Plan B: Further Thoughts on Faith,* reminds us that grace and mercy are often messy but always miraculous. Ann Lamott, *Plan B: Further Thoughts on Faith* (London: Penguin, 2005), 137.
52 *In His Fullness* uses the Hebrew term "davaq" friendships to describe these types of rare friendships between men. However, there are a number of terms in common use today which all describe the same type of unique friendships described by In His Fullness. Paul D. O'Callaghan in *The Feast of Friendship* calls these friendships, "a friendship of virtue" since each man in the friendship finds examples of virtue in the other man which he seeks to attain. Virtuous friendships hold forth untold possibilities of spiritual growth and godliness since the friendship is dedicated to transcendent values and intense devotion to the friend. O'Callaghan, 2002, 36-37. Aelred of Rievaulx calls these types of friendships "Spiritual Friendships" since these bonds between men form a central role in bringing men together in the common pursuit of the one eternal friend, Jesus. These types of friendships, according to Aelred, who wrote his treatise on Spiritual Friendships in the year 1147, begin in Christ, are preserved according to the Spirit of Christ and are perfected in Christ. Aelred of Rievaulx (St) 1147, 51-53. The author will use the term "Spiritual Friendships" throughout this book since it is the original Christian term, and captures the spiritual root of these types of male friendships.

53 Lance Hastings and Jared Feria, *Re-Trek—a Field Guide to Authentic Manhood* (Gainesville: self-published, 2006),38-50.
54 Hastings and Feria, 2006.
55 David Murrow, *The Map: The Way of All Great Men* (Nashville: Thomas Nelson Publishers, 2010). Murrow believes that the three-fold masculine journey of Christ is hidden in the Gospel of Matthew. Christ's journey, which all men must follow, requires learning and integrating the following three virtues into one's life in this order: Submission: being willing to surrender our lives to God and let God lead us through daily communication with God via prayer, discernment and meditation; Strength: embracing the inner courage God has placed in men's hearts to walk through the dark valleys of doubt and crisis and find the deeper truths God is teaching our hearts so that we can then live those truths and teach them by word and example to others on the journey; and Sacrifice: being willing to lay down our lives for Christ and others by placing our highest priority on serving Christ as he might lead us.
56 O'Callaghan 2002, 31. Philia, as developed in Aristotle, has a multileveled reality to it that moved from utility to good virtue. Philia was not seen as a one size fits all reality to the Greeks and the culture that Jesus' message entered. The return to philia may prove to be a helpful concept in the reform of the modern male self-understanding—a move from mere utility (function) to God-inspired good (virtuous) friendship.
57 O'Callaghan 2002, 31. O'Callaghan believes that there are two primary reasons for the decline of friendship as a virtue in our modern era despite the fact that friendships are foundational to most of our lives: first, we live in a society that exalts erotic love as the supreme fulfillment available to human beings and friendship literally has no "sex appeal." Second, friendship does not offer the immediate moral appeal of agape; i.e. we have very few public celebrations or rituals honoring friendships among men.
58 Our heart's deepest desire, St. Augustine teaches, is for God. And we are restless until we find God. St. Augustine of Hippo, *Confessions,* translated by John K. Ryan (New York: Doubleday, 1960) 398. Since one of the ways God reveals God's love for us is through others, perhaps a genuine spiritual friendship which points toward Christ is one way in which God satisfies our heart's desire. See, Song of Songs 3:1-4. "On my bed at night I sought him whom my heart loves. I sought him but did not find him. I will rise then and go about the city; in the streets and crossings I will seek Him whom my heart loves. I sought him but did not find him. The watchmen came upon me as they made their rounds of the city: Have you seen him whom my heart loves? I had hardly left them when I found him

whom my heart loves. I took hold of him and would not let him go...."
Song of Songs 6:12: "Before I knew it my heart had made me one of the blessed."

Chapter Three
59 Nardi 1992, 2.
60 O'Callaghan 2002, 31.
61 Lewis, 1960, 87.
62 Marcus Tullius Cicero, *De Amicitia,* translated by W. Falconer. (New York: Putnam, 1922), 6-20.
63 Cicero 1922, 21-27.
64 Cicero 1922, 21-27.
65 Richard Kraut, "Aristotle's Ethics," *The Stanford Encyclopedia of Philosophy* (Summer 2010) http://plato.stanford.edu/archives/sum2010/entries/aristotle-ethics/.
66 Bennett Helm, "Friendship," *The Stanford Encyclopedia of Philosophy* (July 2009) http://plato.stanford.edu/archives/fall2009/entries/friendship/.
67 Kraut 2010.
68 Kraut 2010.
69 Kraut 2010.
70 A. Moseley, "Philosophy of Love," The Internet Encyclopedia of Philosophy (2010) http://www.iep.utm.edu/love/.
71 Moseley 2010.
72 Moseley 2010.
73 Moseley 2010.
74 Sanderson Beck, *Confucius and Socrates, Teaching Wisdom.* (Santa Barbara: World Peace Communications, 2006), 154-157.
75 Beck 2006, 154-157.
76 Beck 2006, 154-157.
77 Moseley 2010.
78 Moseley 2010.
79 American Heritage Dictionary (Boston: Houghton Mifflin Company, 1978), 1004.
80 O'Callaghan 2002, 49.
81 John 13:23, 19:26, 21:7, 20.
82 John 11:36.
83 Aelred of Rievaulx (St) 1147.
84 O'Callaghan 2002, 13. Dan Steiger, *The Gift of Spiritual Friendship,* http://www.opensourcetheology.net/node/512 (December 15, 2004).
85 Aelred of Rievaulx (St).1147, 65-66.
86 Aelred of Rievaulx (St).1147, 45.
87 Aelred of Rievaulx (St).1147, 104.

88 "Without friends absolutely no life can be happy." Aelred of Rievaulx (St).1147, 110.
89 Aelred of Rievaulx (St).1147, 20-21.
90 Aelred of Rievaulx (St).1147, 53.
91 Aelred of Rievaulx (St).1147, 75.
92 Aelred of Rievaulx (St).1147, 5
93 Aelred of Rievaulx (St).1147, 105.
94 Aelred of Rievaulx (St).1147, 106.
95 Aelred of Rievaulx (St).1147, 105.
96 Aelred of Rievaulx (St).1147, 93.
97 Aelred of Rievaulx (St).1147, 132. When this form of virtuous friendship is gifted to us by God, according to Aelred, "We shall rejoice in the eternal possession of Supreme Goodness; and this friendship, to which here we admit but few, will be outpoured upon all and by all outpoured by God, and God shall be all in all."
98 Aelred of Rievaulx (St).1147, 124-125.
99 In His Fullness, www.inhisfullness.com, a men's ministry which supports the development of healthy male friendships as an alternative to traditional methods of addressing same sex attraction, roots this form of non-exclusive friendship between a man and two to three other men in the term "cleaving love." A cleaving love is filled with mutual affection between two people. It is characterized by fidelity, loyalty, and commitment. Cleaving love is a deep knitting together of heart and soul. It is rooted in truth, honesty and vulnerability and expresses itself through understanding, patience, and a desire to walk with another through the trials of life. It never gives up. It never thinks wrongly of the other. Most of all, it is never sexually motivated. A cleaving love is the kind of love God requires between man and himself. Joshua 23:8. It is the kind of love seen between Ruth and Naomi. Ruth 1:14. It is the kind of love referenced in Proverbs 18:24— "But there is a friend who sticks closer than a brother." See: Jared Feria, *Another Kind of Love* (Gainesville: self-published, 2006), 85, a book on male friendships and love, available through www.inhisfullness.com.
100 Carolinne White, *Christian Friendship in the Fourth Century* (Cambridge: Cambridge University Press, 1992), 55.
101 O'Callaghan 2002, 60.
102 O'Callaghan 2002, 60.
103 White 1992, 63.
104 O'Callaghan 2002, 60.
105 O'Callaghan 2002, 61.
106 O'Callaghan 2002, 61.
107 O'Callaghan 2002, 61.
108 White 1992, 180.

109 O'Callaghan 2002, 61-62.
110 White 1992, 70.
111 O'Callaghan 2002, 69. See: 1 Samuel 18:1, 3-4.
112 Anthony E. Rotundo, "Romantic Friendships: Male Intimacy and Middle-Class Youth in the Northern United States, 1800-1900" *Journal of Social History* (Autumn, 1989), 23: 1.
113 Rotundo 1989, 1.
114 Rotundo 1989, 4.
115 Rotundo 1989, 5 *quoting* James Blake diary, Jan. 5, 1851 and Dec. 31, 1851.
116 Rotundo 1989, 5 *quoting* James Blake diary, Dec. 27, 1851.
117 Rotundo 1989, 5.
118 Rotundo 1989, 2.
119 Rotundo 1989, 2.
120 Rotundo 1989, 2.
121 J. D'Emilio, J. and E. Freedman, E., *Intimate matters: A history of sexuality in America* (New York: Harper and Row, 1099), 121.
122 Nardi 1992, 3.
123 Rotundo 1989, 10.
124 Nardi 1992, 2.
125 Nardi 1992, 44.
126 Rotundo 1989, 5.
127 Nardi 1992, 3.
128 Nardi 1992, 3.

Chapter Four
129 See generally, Bly 1990 and Murrow 2010.
130 Aelred of Rievaulx (St).1147, 40.
131 Aelred of Rievaulx (St).1147, 40.
132 Aelred of Rievaulx (St).1147, 40.
133 Nardi 1992, 2.
134 O'Callaghan 2002, 145-146.
135 O'Callaghan 2002, 145-146.
136 O'Callaghan 2002, 145-146.
137 Bly 1990, 2.
138 Bly 1990, 49.
139 Bly 1990, 49.
140 Nardi 1992, 2.
141 Arnold 1995, 51.
142 Bly 1990, 46.
143 Flinders 2000, 138-145.
144 Bly 1990, 49-50.
145 Bly 1990, 50.

Chapter Five

146 A hilarious rendition of the man rules appears on the Website: *MIStupid. Com—The Online Knowledge Magazine,* http://www.mistupid.com/people/page024.htm, (November 25, 2011) and is reprinted below:

1. Thou shall not rent the movie *Chocolate*.
2. Under no circumstances may 2 men share an umbrella.
3. Any man who brings a camera to a bachelor party may be legally killed and eaten by his fellow partygoers.
4. When you are queried by a buddy's wife, girlfriend, mother, father, priest, shrink, dentist, accountant, or dog walker, you need not and should not provide any useful information whatsoever as to his whereabouts. You are permitted to deny his very existence.
5. Unless he murdered someone in your immediate family, you must bail a friend out of jail within 12 hours.
6. You may exaggerate any anecdote told in a bar by 50% without recrimination; beyond that, anyone within earshot is allowed to call B*LLSH$T. (Exception: When trying to pick up a girl, the allowable exaggeration rate rises to 400%).
7. If you've known a guy for more than 24 hours, his sister is off-limits forever.
8. The minimum amount of time you have to wait for another guy who's running late is 5 minutes. For a girl, you are required to wait 10 minutes for every point of hotness she scores on the classic 1-10 babe scale.
9. Complaining about the brand of free beer in a buddy's refrigerator is forbidden. You may gripe if the temperature is unsuitable.
10. No man is ever required to buy a birthday present for another man. In fact, even remembering a friend's birthday is strictly optional and slightly gay.
11. Agreeing to distract the ugly friend of a hot babe that your buddy is trying to hook up with is your legal duty. Should you get carried away with your good deed and end up having sex with the beast, your pal is forbidden to speak of it, even at your bachelor party.
12. Before dating a buddy's "ex", you are required to ask his permission and he in return is required to grant it.
13. Women who claim they "love to watch sports" must be treated as spies until they demonstrate knowledge of the game and the ability to pick a buffalo wing clean.
14. If a man's zipper is down, that's his problem - you didn't see nothin'.
15. The universal compensation for buddies who help you move is beer.

16. A man must never own a cat or like his girlfriend's cat.
17. When stumbling upon other guys watching a sports event, you may always ask the score of the game in progress, but you may never ask who's playing.
18. When your girlfriend/wife expresses a desire to fix her whiney friend up with your pal, you may give her the go-ahead only if you'll be able to warn your buddy and give him time to prepare excuses about joining the priesthood.
19. It is permissible to consume a fruity chick drink only when you're sunning on a tropical beach... and it's delivered by a topless supermodel... and it's free.
20. Unless you're in prison, never fight naked.
21. A man in the company of a hot, suggestively dressed woman must remain sober enough to fight.
22. If a buddy is outnumbered, out manned, or too drunk to fight, you must jump into the fight. Exception: If within the last 24 hours his actions have caused you to think, "What this guy needs is a good ass-whoopin", then you may sit back and enjoy.
23. Phrases that may NOT be uttered to another man while weight lifting: "Yeah, baby, push it!", "C'mon, give me one more! Harder!", "Another set and we can hit the showers." "Nice ass, are you a Sagittarius?"
24. Never hesitate to reach for the last beer or the last slice of pizza, but not both. That's just plain mean.
25. If you compliment a guy on his six-pack, you better be referring to his beer.
26. Never join your girlfriend/wife in dissing a buddy, except when she's withholding sex pending your response.
27. Never talk to a man in the bathroom unless you're on equal footing: either both urinating or both waiting in line. In all other situations, a nod is all the conversation you need.
28. Unlocking a car door for another man is polite. Opening it is gay.

147 Nardi 1992, 1-2.
148 Nardi 1992, 2.
149 Nardi 1992, 2.
150 Michael A. Messner, *Like Family: Power, Intimacy and Sexuality in Male Athlete's Friendship,* reprinted in *Men's Friendships,* edited by Peter M. Nardi (Newbury Park: Sage Publications 1992), 215-237. While sports/team centered relationships for men can be limiting to the deepening of men's relationships, there is an interesting theory that suggests the world of sport provides a nearly complete theology and helpful ongoing "gospel"

that allows men to touch intimate spiritual topics like sin, resurrection, death, new creation, salvation, redemption, etc. via the ongoing sports narrative. From this perspective sports can be used as a starting place for a positive upgrade in male intimacy rather than a whipping boy to be criticized. See for example: Father John McCloskey, *Friendship: The Key to Evangelization of Men,* http://www.catholicity.com/mccloskey/friendship.html (May 2004).
151 Messner 1992, 232.
152 Messner 1992, 232-233.
153 "F.I.N.E." is a song by the American hard rock band, Aerosmith. The song title, "F.I.N.E." is an acronym for "**F**— - - **U**p, **I**nsecure, **N**eurotic, and **E**motional" as stated in the album's liner notes. Steven Tyler and Joe Perry. *F.I.N.E.: Pump.* Geffen: September 1989.
154 Arnold 1995, 180-199. See for example, John 11:35 where Jesus comes face to face with the death of his friend Lazarus and John writes, "Jesus wept." It has been remarked that this is the shortest verse in the Bible; but it is exceedingly important. It shows Jesus as a tender and vulnerable friend, and evinces his character as a man. And from this we learn: that the most tender personal friendship is not inconsistent with the most pure religion. Piety binds stronger the ties of friendship, makes more tender the emotions of love, and seals and sanctifies the affections of friends. Contrast this tender characterization of Jesus' personality as a man with his strength in Matthew 21:12 where he physically throws out the moneychangers from the temple and kicks over their tables.

Chapter 6
155 Lewis 1960.
156 Arnold 1995, 1.
157 Proverbs 27:17.
158 Arnold 1995, 1.
159 Hastings and Feria 2006, 50.
160 Stu Weber, *Locking Arms: God's Design for Masculine Friendships* (Sisters, Oregon: Questar Publishers, 1995).
161 Hastings and Feria 2006, 50.
162 Tom McGrath, "Is men's spirituality out of the woods? Beyond the banging drums and clashing symbols, Catholic men have a lot to gain from tapping into an authentic men's spirituality movement," T*he Free Library,* http://www.thefreelibrary.com/Is men's spirituality out of the woods? Beyond the banging drums and . . .-a0844344952 (April 1, 2002). For a good summary of recent publications on the men's movement and men's spirituality see also: Michael J. Farrell, "Men in search of their souls: in recent books, the quest for the male-spirituality grail is producing

decidedly mixed results," *The Free Library,* http://www.thefreelibrary.com/Men in search of their souls: in recent books, the guest for the...-a084344970 (April 1, 2002), (accessed July 12, 2011).

163 McGrath 2002.
164 McGrath 2002.
165 McGrath 2002.
166 McGrath 2002.
167 McGrath 2002. According to Richard Rohr, author of numerous books on men's spirituality and male liberation, including *From Wild Man to Wise Man—Reflections on Male Spirituality,* (Richard Rohr, *From Wild Man to Wise Man—Reflections on Male Spirituality* (Cincinnati: St. Anthony Messenger Press, 2005)), "Possibly the most urgent change needed in our churches is the restoration of some meaningful form of authentic, experiential initiation of young men in the church. Men in almost all cultures are not born, they are made. The boy has to be separated from protective feminine energy, led into ritual space where newness and maleness can be experienced as holy. Then the boy must be ritually wounded and tested and experience bonding with other men and loyalty to the culture's values." Rohr 2005, 31-36.
168 For more information see: http://www.malespirituality.org/rites_of_passage.htm.
169 See: http://www.nfcm.net/
170 For an example of a men's ministry group using this form of prayer and fellowship see: http://www.goovertheedge.com/mens_spirituality_group/.
171 Nelson 1988, 63. According to Nelson, "Most men feel that genital sex is the supreme intimacy between people, and if this is true, normal men cannot have intimate male friends. This distortion in thinking leads to the theme sounded time and time again that a large segment of my feelings about other men are unknown or distorted because I am afraid they might have something to do with homosexuality. Now I'm lonely for other men and don't know how to find what I want with them."

Chapter 7

172 Proverbs 27:17.
173 Nelson 1988, 13. Nelson suggests that because of the distortion of masculinity in our culture men are hurting and don't understand why. This hurting he describes as "Our yearning for emotional intimacy with other males—sons, fathers, and friends—yet finding ourselves unprepared, unequipped, and fearful of that intimacy. The hurt is our wanting relationships of genuine equality and mutuality with women, yet finding ourselves crippled by centuries of male sexism and by our

emotional dependencies on the opposite sex. The hurt is in our discovery that we have bought heavily into the message that our self-worth is directly dependent upon our occupational success, and yet the idol of work somehow does not deliver its promised salvation."

174 Helm 2009.
175 Pable 1966, 1, 19.
176 Aelred of Rievaulx (St) 1147, 92-93. Since the foundation of spiritual friendship is the love of God, a friend ought to be chosen with utmost care and tested with extreme caution warns Aelred of Rievaulx.
177 John 13:23; 19:26; 21:7, 20.
178 O'Callaghan 1992, 52.
179 O'Callaghan 1992, 49.
180 O'Callaghan 1992, 53.
181 John 13:23.
182 John 19:25–27.
183 O'Callaghan 1992, 53.
184 Bly 1990, 93.
185 John 13:22-25: "One of the disciples, the one Jesus loved dearly, was reclining against him, his head on his shoulder."
186 Luke 22:14-16: "When it was time, he sat down, all the apostles with him, and said, 'You've no idea how much I have looked forward to eating this Passover meal with you before I enter my time of suffering. It's the last one I'll eat until we all eat it together in the kingdom of God.'"
187 John 19:26–27.
188 O'Callaghan 1992, 53.
189 John 16:25-33.
190 O'Callaghan 1992, 55.
191 John 1:40-42.
192 1 Samuel 18:1: "[When Jonathan met David for the first time] an immediate bond was forged between them. He became totally committed to David. From that point on he would be David's number-one advocate and friend."
193 Matt 16:13-20.
194 Matt 16:13-20.
195 Matt 16:13-20.
196 Matt 17:5-8.
197 Judith Bleich 1983, 25-26. "The Symbols in Innovative Rituals." Sh'ma, a Journal of Jewish Responsibility. December 23, 1983.
198 John 13:3-6: "So [Jesus] got up from the supper table, set aside his robe, and put on an apron. Then he poured water into a basin and began to wash the feet of his disciples, drying them with his apron."
199 John 13:7-12.

End Notes

200 John 14:15-27.
201 Aelred of Rievaulx (St) 1147, 23.
202 John 11: 14-15.
203 John 11:15.
204 2 Cor 12:10.
205 O'Callaghan 1992, 50.
206 O'Callaghan 1992, 50.
207 1 Samuel 13:13-14.
208 Isaiah 41:8.
209 O'Callaghan 1992, 50-51.
210 O'Callaghan 1992, 137.
211 O'Callaghan 1992, 137.
212 Anne Robertson, *God with Skin On: Finding God's Love in Human Relationships* (Harrisburg: Morehouse Publishing, 2009).
213 O'Callaghan 1992, 137-138.
214 O'Callaghan 1992, 137-138.
215 Pavel Florensky, *The Pillar and Ground of the Truth* (Princeton: Princeton University Press, 1977) 327-330.
216 A sample ritual entitled, "Order for Making Brothers," is attached to this paper as Appendix 1.
217 O'Callaghan 1992, 13, 73-87, 138.
218 O'Callaghan 1992, 101.
219 O'Callaghan 1992, 53.
220 Richard J. Hauser, S.J, Moving in the Spirit---Becoming a Contemplative in Action (New York: Paulist Press, 1986), 26-27.
221 Belden C. Lane, *Landscapes of the Sacred* (Baltimore: John Hopkins University Press, 2002), 19.
222 1 Samuel 18:1-4.
223 John 1:40-42.
224 www.inhisfullness.com.
225 Aelred of Rievaulx (St.) 1147, 92-93.
226 Aelred of Rievaulx (St.) 1147, 105.
227 Aelred of Rievaulx (St.) 1147, 105.
228 From the song by Joe Wise entitled Maleita's Song: I'm in love with my God. http://www.joeandmaleitawise.com.
229 Keith R. Anderson and Randy Reese, *Spiritual Mentoring* (Downers Grove: Intervarsity Press, 1999), 19.
230 John 17:20-23.
231 Anderson and Reese 1999, 13, 15.
232 Anderson and Reese 1999, 16.
233 Matt 28:19-20.
234 Catechism of the Catholic Church, 1994, #293.

235   John 14:20; 17:20-22.
236   John 15:13.

Chapter 8
237   Thomas Merton, *Spiritual Direction and Meditation* (Collegeville, Minn: Order of St. Benedict Press, 1960), 16.
238   www.dominicancenter.com

Bibliography

American Heritage Dictionary (Boston: Houghton Mifflin Company, 1978).

Anderson, Keith R. and Randy Reese., *Spiritual Mentoring* (Downers Grove: Intervarsity Press, 1999).

Arnold, Patrick M. *Wildmen, Warriors and Kings* (New York: The Crossroad Publishing Company, 1995).

Augustine, Saint. *Confessions,* translated by John K. Ryan (New York: Doubleday, 1960).

Beck, Sanderson. *Confucius and Socrates: Teaching Wisdom* (Santa Barbara: World Peace Communications, 2006).

Bleich, Judith. "The Symbols in Innovative Rituals," *Sh'ma—a Journal of Jewish Responsibility* (December 23, 1983).

Bly, Robert. *Iron John: A Book About Men* (Cambridge: Da Cappa Press, 1990).

Buber, Martin. "Distance and Relation." *The Hibbert Journal* (January 1951).

Carnagey, Glen. "A Study of the Hebrew Word Davaq," h*ttp://www.realtime.net/wdoud/topics/union.html*, (2010).

Catechism of the Catholic Church, 1994.

Cedeno, Ken. "Is God Dead?" *Time* (April 8, 1966).

Cicero, Marcus Tullius. *De Amiciti* (New York: Putnam, 1922).

D'Emilio, J. and E. Freedman *Intimate matters: A history of sexuality in America* (New York: Harper and Row, 1988).

Eldredge, John. *Wild at Heart.* (Nashville: Thomas Nelson Press, 2001).

Farrell, Michael J., "Men in search of their souls: in recent books, the guest for the male-spirituality grail is producing decidedly mixed results," *The Free Library* http://www.thefreelibrary.com/Men in search of their souls: in recent books, the guest for the...-a084344970 (April, 1, 2002).

Feria, Jared and Lance Hastings. *Another Kind of Love* (Gainesville: Self-Published, 2006).

Feria, Jared and Lance Hastings. *Re-Trek: a Field Guide to Authentic Manhood* (Gainesville: Self-Published, 2006).

Fields, Suzanne. "When Manly Virtue Died," *The Grand Rapids Press*, 22 November 2011.

Flinders, Carol Lee. *Rebalancing the World* (New York: HarperCollins Publishers, 2000).

Florensky, Pavel. *The Pillar and Ground of the Truth* (Princeton: Princeton University Press, 1977).

Halper, Jan. *Quiet Desperation: The Truth About Successful Men* (New York: Warner Books, 1988).

Hauser, Richard J., S.J. *Moving in the Spirit—Becoming a Contemplative in Action.* (New York: Paulist Press, 1986).

Helm, Bennet. "Friendship." The Stanford Encyclopedia of Philosophy. http://plato/standford.edu/arrchives/fall2009/entries/friendship/. (Fall 2009).

Hodgson, Boyson. "The New Macho."http://journeytomanhood.blogspot.com/2010/10/new-macho.html (Man-Making Blog 2010).

Kraut, Richard. "Aristotle's Ethics." The Stanford Encylopedia of Philosophy. http://plato.stanford.edu/archives/summer2010/entries/aristotle-ethics/. (Summer 2010).

Lamont, Ann. *Plan B: Further Thoughts on Faith* (London: Penguin, 2005).

Lane, Belden, C. *Landscapes of the Sacred* (Baltimore: John Hopkins University Press, 2002).

Lewis, C.S. *The Four Loves* (New York: Harvest/HBJ Books, 1960).

McCloskey, Father John, *Friendship: The Key to Evangelization of Men,* http://www.catholicity.com/mccloskey/friendship.html (May 2004).

McGrath, Tom. "Is Men's Spirituality Out of the Woods?" http://www.thefreelibrary.com/Is men's spirituality out of the woods? Beyond the banging drums and...-a084344952. (2002).

McGuire, Brian Patrick. *Friendship and Community: The Monastic Experience* (Ithaca: Cornell University Press, 2010).

Merton, Thomas. *Spiritual Direction and Meditation* (Collegeville: Order of St. Benedict Press, 1960).

Messener, Michael. Like Family: Power, Intimacy and Sexuality in Male Athlete Friendships (Newbury Park: Sage Publications, 1992).

Moseley, A. "Philosophy of Love." The Internet Encyclopedia of Philosophy http://www/iep/utm.edu/love/.

Murrow, David, W*hy Men Hate Going to Church* (Nashville: Thomas Nelson Press, 2005).

Murrow, David. *The Map: The Way of All Great Men (*Nashville: Thomas Nelson Press, 2010).

Nardi, Peter M. *Men's Friendships: Research on Men and Masculinities* (Newbury Park: Sage Publications, 1988).

Nelson, James B. The Intimate Connection: Male Sexuality, Masculine Spirituality (Philadephia: Westminster Press, 1988).

O'Callaghan, Paul D. *The Feast of Friendship* (Wichita: Eight Day Press, 2002).

Pable, Martin. *The Quest for the Male Soul* (Notre Dame: Ave Marie Press, 1966).

Reese, Randy and Keith R. Anderson. *Spiritual Mentoring* (Downers Grove: InterVarsity Press, 1999).

Rievaulx, Aelred of, *Spiritual Friendship (*Kalamazoo: Cistercian Press, 1147).

Robertson, Anne, *God with Skin On: Finding God's Love in Human Relationships* (Harrisburg: Morehouse Publishing , 2009).

Rohr, Richard. From Wild Man to Wise Man—Reflections on Male Spirituality (Cincinnati: St. Anthony Messenger, 2005).

Rohr, Richard. On the Threshold Of Transformation (Chicago: Loyola Press, 2010).
Rosin, Hanna. "The End of Men." *The Atlantic*, July/August 2010.
Rotundo, Anthony. "Romantic Friendships: Male Intimacy and Middle-class Youth in the Northern United States." *Journal of Social History*, Autumn 1989: 23:1.
Sayles, Matt. "Men's Lib." *Newsweek*, September 20, 2010.
Steiger, Dan, *The Gift of Spiritual Friendship*, http://www.opensourcetheology.net/node/512 (December 15, 2004).
Walstrom, Mark. "Men's Spirituality: Discovering our Myths and Remembering Ourselves." http://www.markwalstrom.com/articles/mens-spirituality.html (2010).
Weber, Stu. *Locking Arms: God's Design for Masculine Friendships* (Sisters, Oregon: Questar Publishers, 1995).
White, Carolinne. *Christian Friendship in the Fourth Century* (Cambridge: Cambridge University Press, 1992).

About the Author

Brian J. Plachta is an attorney with a full-time law practice in Grand Rapids, Michigan. He is married and he and his wife Denise just celebrated their 28th wedding anniversary. He has four adult children: Matthew, Daniel, Stephen, and Mary Claire.

In addition to his law career, Brian holds a Master of Pastoral Counseling degree and is a certified Spiritual Director. Brian is a frequent workshop speaker on men's spirituality topics for churches, spiritual life centers, and men's conferences throughout the State of Michigan. He has been interviewed on numerous occasions by local media, including The Grand Rapids Press and WGVSU-Radio, as an expert on men's topics. He serves as an adjunct faculty member at the Dominican Center at Marywood, an ecumenical spiritual life center in West Michigan.

In addition to *Pillars of Steel*, Brian has authored: *To Ease the Pain—Remembering My Father on the Masculine Journey*; and *Manarchy: Having the Balls to Break the Man Code*. Brian has taught and created numerous men's spirituality workshops, which include: *Listening for God Knows What—How God Speaks to Men in Unique Ways*; *Men's Health—Finding the Wild Goose Within*; *Men's Group Spiritual Direction*; *Fathered by God*; and *A Man's Spiritual Toolbox—Discovering the Tools for Balance & Wholeness*. He has also created and conducted numerous men's retreat experiences including: *Journey into Nature—A Man's Pathway toward Hearing the Voice of God*; and *A Morning of Reflection and Conversation on Men's Spirituality*.

His website (www.goovertheedge.com) and blog (www.manarchy.org) contain practical advice and input for men on how to embrace their masculine gifts and grow spiritually on their God-path. His non-profit men's ministry group, Over the Edge, has been recognized by the Roman Catholic Diocese of Grand Rapids as a vital lay ministry assisting in the development of men's wholeness and spirituality.

About the Author

Brian earned his Juris Doctorate degree from the University of Detroit-Mercy School of Law in 1983. His Master of Pastoral Counseling degree was awarded by the Graduate Theological Foundation in May 2012. Brian has also completed his studies as a deacon candidate through the Diocese of Grand Rapids. A lifelong learner, he has taken on-going theological courses at Western Theological Seminary in Holland, Michigan, and Creighton University in Omaha, Nebraska. He completed the five year program for spiritual direction and has been certified as a Spiritual Director by the Dominican Center at Marywood. He regularly meets with men one-on-one for individual spiritual direction and facilitates several men's group spiritual direction circles. He lives in the northeast end of Grand Rapids, Michigan, with his wife, his dog, Riley, and his wife's cat, Rascal (Brian claims no ownership of the cat). He and his wife have just become empty-nesters having successfully launched their fourth child into college. Denise is glad Brian is pursuing a second career as a writer since she says, "He always needs another mountain to climb."

WHAT OTHERS ARE SAYING ABOUT
PILLARS OF STEEL

When I was in college, my dad kissed me on the lips as he dropped me off at my dorm. At that time, I didn't think anything of it—it was normal—an everyday occurrence.

"What are you lookin' at?" I said to my roommate who glared back at me in shock as my dad walked away. Because of that kiss, I got kicked out of the "man club" at a pretty early age, never to return. Now, some thirty years later I have finally found validation as a man from the words of *Pillars of Steel*—thank you!

—Ralph M Annunziata
Global Creative Director
NUNZdesigns
Chicago, Illinois